L B

THE OFFICIAL LONDON TRANSPORT GUIDE TO ENJOYING A SHORT STAY IN LONDON

LONDON TRANSPORT

London Breaks by **Jenny Ward**

Published jointly by **London Transport, 55 Broadway, Westminster, London SW1** and **Book Production Consultants, 47 Norfolk Street, Cambridge CB1 2LE**

Published 1991.
© London Transport and Book Production Consultants 1991.
ISBN 1 871829 07 0

A CIP catalogue record for this book is available from the British Library.

Whilst every effort has been made to ensure the accuracy of the information contained in this book, the publishers can take no responsibility for possible errors or omissions, and readers should note that changes in admission and travel details occur from time to time. The inclusion of a building or open space in this publication does not necessarily imply the right of entry. The opinions expressed are those of the author and are not necessarily those of the publishers.

Enquiries regarding advertising in future editions of this and other guides in the series should be addressed to **Book Production Consultants, 47 Norfolk Street, Cambridge CB1 2LE.**

Other Guides in the series:
Budget London
Family London
Royal & Historic London

The publishers would like to thank the following for their permission to reproduce photographs: pp.13, 26, 28, 44, 69, David Phillips; pp.17 (top), 47, 52, 56-7, 77, 78, 79, J C Mervyn Blatch; p.17 (bottom), Harrods Limited; p.18, Liberty Retail Limited; p.25, Woodmansterne Picture Library; pp.27, 37, 38, London Transport Museum; p.29 The Savoy Group; p.53, The Royal Tournament; p. 58, London Tourist Board; p. 71, Zoo Operations Limited; p. 75, Imperial War Museum.

Design and production by **Book Production Consultants**

Cover design by **Peter Dolton**
Book design by **Peter Dolton**
Illustrations by **John York**
Maps by **FWT, London N19**
Film origination by **Anglia Graphics, Bedford**
Printed and bound in the United Kingdom by **Staples Printers (Kettering) Ltd.**

CONTENTS

INTRODUCTION

Ships, towers, domes, theatres, and temples lie
Open unto the fields, and to the sky;

wrote Wordsworth on a visit to London
one day in September 1802. Nearly two hundred
years later the skyline displays shapes he would not be
able to identify, but many of the things he did see remain.
There are even traces of the fields he glimpsed from
Westminster Bridge in place-names such as Lincoln's Inn
Fields. London is ever changing, but one thing that does
not change is the abundance of things to see
and enjoy that it offers to visitors.

The four official London Transport guides – *Royal &
Historic London, Budget London, Family London* and
London Breaks – are designed for the visitor to London
who has little time to spare. To get the most out of a short
stay or day trip, choose the book that best suits your
pocket and your needs. *Royal & Historic London* is the
one for those who particularly want to see the traditional
places and events. *Budget London* has lots of suggestions
for enjoying yourself with the minimum outlay; it takes in
all the major tourist attractions in doing that. *Family
London* offers ideas for all ages – and if your group
includes someone who is disabled, note that the walks in
it contain specific information for wheelchair users. All the
guides include a Disabled in London section with transport advice.

London Breaks is designed for the visitor who is able
to stay for a few days. It can stand on its own or be used
in conjunction with one of the other books. The first section, on the West End, covers the most popular locations
for the visitor and is mainly concerned with shops,
theatres, pubs and entertainment. The second section,
Events month by month, lists traditional events. The set-
tings of most of these are places of interest in themselves
and are described in this and the other guides. If you
would like admission times and prices for these, *Royal &
Historic London, Budget London* and *Family London*
have the details for the eighty most visited locations in the

capital. The Parks and gardens section and the Sport section are both aimed at diverting the visitor from the crowded central areas of the West End and the City into the quieter spots traditionally enjoyed by Londoners.

The Accommodation section is based on the guide published annually by the London Tourist Board (LTB) and lists small hotels chosen for their proximity to places mentioned not just in *London Breaks*, but also in the other titles.

Demolition of the long-established Criterion theatre reinforces the point that change is constant in London, so please try not to be disappointed if a restaurant has vanished by the time you arrive outside hungry or if an enticing museum has decided to close on Mondays on the very Monday when you visit. There are

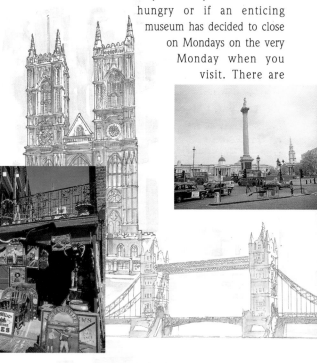

attractions to compensate. The best way to avoid disruption of your plans is to check opening times a few days before you plan to visit – use the telephone numbers in this and the other guides. It would also be worth consulting the daily papers and specialist weeklies such as *Time Out, City Limits* and *What's On.*

In this guide there are two maps. The one near the beginning shows the central area. At the end there is a pull-out map giving you a comprehensive view of the capital city. There are so many things to see in a short distance in central London that sometimes there is too much detail to be shown clearly in the space available on the maps. You will find it useful to have a copy of a detailed plan such as the *London A to Z* to consult as well.

For general tourist information in office hours the London Tourist Board has a helpline on 071-730 3488. For travel enquiries dial London Transport on 071-222 1234, or Travelcheck (for recorded, up-to-the-minute information) on 071-222 1200. If you are dialling from a number with the same prefix as the one you need, leave out the prefix. Each of these numbers has a queuing system; if you re-dial you lose your place, so hang on if you don't get a reply at first.

Above all, enjoy your stay, and welcome to London.

KEY

U   Nearest Underground station

BR   Nearest British Rail station

DLR   Nearest Docklands Light Railway station

D   Access for the disabled

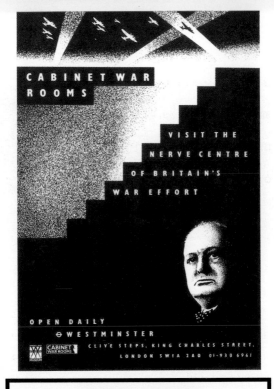

While you're seeing the sights in Britain don't forget the folks back home. In any language a postcard is the brightest, quickest and simplest way to say Hi!

They take seconds to write and arrive at their destination in no time at all. They are also great value.

Stamps are available in handy books of four which you can carry with you wherever you travel.

Pick up a book from post offices or anywhere you see the Royal Mail Stockist signs.

P.S. *Want to say more? Or say it more personally? Then send a colourful new pictorial aerogramme, available from post offices.*

Royal Mail

International

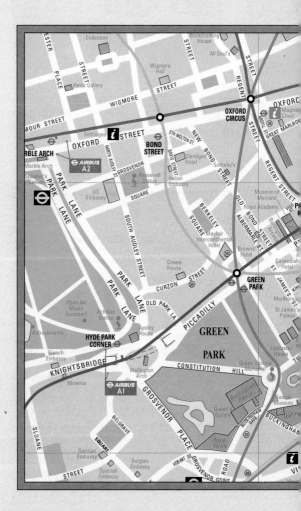

ST JAMES'S
MAYFAIR
SOHO
COVENT GARDEN
LEICESTER SQUARE

AROUND THE WEST END

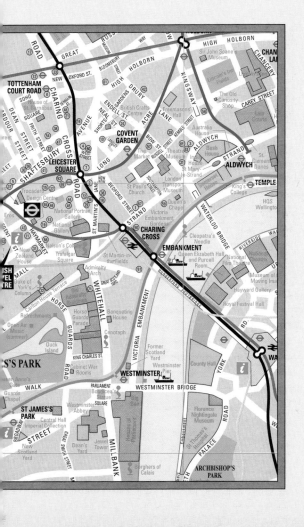

ST JAMES'S

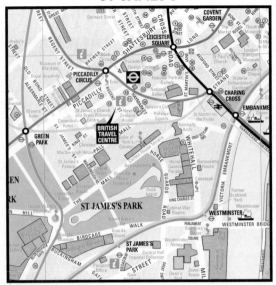

The West End developed from the area around West-minster Abbey and the Palace of Westminster as the aristocracy clustered round the monarch that they de-pended on for a living. It gradually nudged north when Henry VIII established his Court at the Palace of Whitehall but it was in the reign of Charles II that the West End as we know it took form. Charles also held his Court at Whitehall, where he died ('Don't let poor Nelly starve'), and laid out St James's Park. But the area north of the park was developed by Henry Jermyn, 1604-84, Earl of St Albans.

Jermyn was a faithful servant of Charles I, and then managed the affairs of his widow, Henrietta Maria, as Master of the House. He served Charles II as an elder statesman and, putting his faith in property, founded the West End when he bought the 45 acres of St James's Fields and began to build. Before then there were only the Palace of St James, built on an old leper hospital, and a few houses.

Jermyn Street and **King Street** were the first streets he built, in 1667 and 1673, when Piccadilly was an insig-nificant thoroughfare. So the new parish church of St James

St James's Park

was designed by Wren to face southwards to Jermyn Street, though approached normally today from Piccadilly.

Pall Mall got its name from a game similar to croquet and its most famous early resident was Nell Gwyn, at Number 79, perhaps on the site of the Reform Club. The present line of earls of St Albans owes its existence to the death of the heirless Henry Jermyn and the birth of a royal son to Nell. It was only in the time of the Regency that Pall Mall achieved the architectural elegance it now possesses at the hands of Beau Nash. Here are the Travellers' Club, the Reform Club and the unmarked Athenaeum. A member of the House of Lords once told me that the Athenaeum was the 'second-best club in town' – the House being the first.

Clubland had its gambling origins in St James's Street in the eighteenth century with clubs like Crockford's (where the Duke of Wellington was a member), White's (the oldest), Brook's, Boodle's and Almack's – the last named admitted men and women. Writer David Benedictus' story of the street tells us that here the men nominated and voted for the women, and vice versa.

FROM TOP TO TOE

The predominance of moneyed men in the area meant shops to cater for their tastes. Lock's hatters started out at Number 6 St James's Street over 250 years ago and later the bowler began life here. Wellington bought his boots at Hoby's, and Churchill bought his cigars at Robert Lewis. Berry's (founded in the 1690s) began to weigh their customers on the tea and coffee scales as they bought their wines and so now today we can find out how much Byron weighed, or the Prince Regent, if we think the information might ever be of use.

Christie's, the fine art and furniture auctioneers in King Street, was founded by James Christie, a Scot born in 1730, who started the auction house after leaving the navy.

The Cavendish Hotel, in Jermyn Street, now rebuilt, was run before the First World War by Rosa Lewis, the 'Duchess of Duke Street'. The Cavendish had a discreet back entrance in Duke Street which guests' guests could use. The Prince of Wales (Edward VII, not Prince Charles) was one of her favoured clients. Daughter of an under-taker, she began her working life in humble domestic service and worked her way up to a career catering – in the widest sense of the word – to the gentry. Portraits of her hang on the staircase of the hotel and the downstairs bar is called the 'Sub Rosa'.

Floris is in Jermyn Street, purveyor of English flower perfumes since George IV. Here too is a Spaghetti House, for reliable fare. If you prefer bread and cheese for lunch, try Paxton and Whitfield for cheeses.

RITZ AND POOR

Piccadilly eventually picked itself up out of the gutter. Yet I saw a poor wretch sitting in the shade of the Ritz hoping for handouts. Either that or he was a reclusive millionaire looking for a kind person to leave his millions to. In the old days tea in the Palm Court of the Ritz was no problem, but today booking well in advance is essential. Try the St James's Restaurant at Fortnum and Mason's instead, further along the street. The store is famed for its hampers and groceries. To the English living abroad Fortnum's is the essence of England. Visit on the hour to see Mr Fortnum and Mr Mason bow to each other on the chime of the clock above the door. (While away the time to the chime in Hatchard's bookshop a few doors away.)

Eating and drinking

(££ = up to £15 for one, £££ = up to £25 for one, ££££ = the very special places)
Le Caprice, Arlington House, Arlington Street, SW1
071-629 2239, £££-££££
Franco's, 61-63 Jermyn Street, SW1
071-493 3645, ££££
Jules Bar, 85 Jermyn Street, SW1
071-930 4700, ££
Spaghetti House, 74-76 Duke Street, W1
071-629 6097, ££
Spaghetti House, 16-17 Jermyn Street, SW1
071-734 7334, ££
Suntory Restaurant, 72-73 St James's Street, SW1
071-409 0201 (Japanese), ££££

MAYFAIR

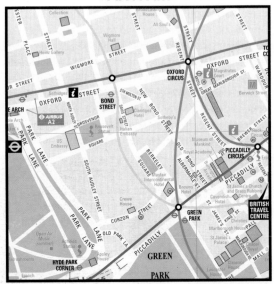

Mayfair begins on the north side of Piccadilly. **Oxford Street** forms its northern boundary with **Park Lane** and plush hotels to the west, and **Regent Street** to the east. After Jermyn set the fashion for development, he was followed by others like Sir Thomas Bond, whose names live on in the streets they built. **Berkeley Square**, where the nightingale sang, provides a cluster of interest. Here is Annabel's at Number 44, an exclusive nightclub with the brightest of royalty, aristocracy and stars as members. Membership is difficult. Langan's Brasserie in **Stratton Street** may give a better opportunity for star hunting, especially upstairs.

Also in Stratton Street is the Mayfair Hotel. Their Candlelight Room was famous in the 1930s for its Big Band broadcasting with Ambrose and Harry Roy. The ballroom was converted to the Mayfair theatre in the 1960s and the hotel now lists both the theatre and the Crystal Ballroom among its attractions.

The quiet Brown's Hotel, between **Dover** and **Albemarle Streets**, was founded by Lord Byron's valet in 1837. This was used as 'Bertram's Hotel' in the BBC's Agatha Christie series with Joan Hickson as Miss Marple.

Down at the **Hyde Park Corner** end of the street find

the Hard Rock Cafe, or for a quieter meal, L'Artiste Musclé in Shepherd Market, my favourite bistro.

SPARING NO EXPENSE

The Roux brothers own Le Gavroche, at 43 **Upper Brook Street**, round the corner from the United States Embassy. Here an average dinner costs a fortune and is probably worth it. (I say 'probably' because I can't afford to eat there.) Further along **Brook Street** itself is Claridges, a hotel which does not need to advertise.

Regent Street

Foreign royalty stay here, assured of faultless service, near Chanel, Gucci, Yves St Laurent, Tiffany, Hermès, Cardin and all the top names in **Old Bond Street** and **New Bond Street**. (Sloane Street, Brompton Road – for Harrods – and Beauchamp Place are the stamping grounds of others, including

Harrods

those about to rise to the top.) Widow Applebaum's in the pedestrianised **South Molton Street** is the place to watch the world go by over a coffee.

By now tatty **Oxford Street** is looming on the northern horizon. The popularity of this street is quite amazing. Why go to the middle of London to shop in high street

Liberty

stores? Why not just shop in the high street? The exception is Selfridges, a world of its own. Otherwise Oxford Street does not invite. **Regent Street** is built more on a human scale. Liberty, built with wood salvaged from old ships, has judged the 'people space' exactly right; not too cramped, not too cavernous. Other traditional names line Regent Street, like Aquascutum, Dickins and Jones, Garrard – the Crown jewellers – and near **Piccadilly Circus** the Café Royal, now Trust House Forte, but once the haunt of Oscar Wilde, James McNeil Whistler and the Edwardian set.

Clubs and discos

Annabel's, 44 Berkeley Square, W1
071-629 3558
Legends, 29 Old Burlington Street, W1
071-437 9933
Prohibition, 9 Hanover Street, W1
071-493 0689
The Stork Club, 99 Regent Street, W1
071-734 3686/1393
Wall Street, 14 Bruton Place, W1
071-493 0630
Xenon, 196 Piccadilly, W1
071-734 9344

Eating and drinking

(£ = up to £5 for one, ££ = up to £15 for one, £££ = up to £25 for one, ££££ = the very special places)
L'Artiste Musclé, Shepherd Market
071-493 6150, ££
Café Royal, 68 Regent Street, W1
071-437 9090, ££££

Le Gavroche, 43 Upper Brook Street, W1
071-408 0881/499 1826, ££££
The Granary, 39 Albemarle Street, W1
071-493 2978, £
Hard Rock Cafe, 150 Old Park Lane, W1
071-629 0382, ££
Langan's Brasserie, Stratton Street, W1
071-493 6437/491 8822, £££
Pizza on the Park, 11-13 Knightsbridge, SW1
(just beyond Hyde Park Corner tube station)
071-235 5273/5550 (live jazz), ££
Wheeler's, 1-4 South Molton Street, W1
071-629 2471 (fish), £££

SOHO

Soho is roughly the area between Regent Street and Charing Cross Road south of Oxford Street. An exploration might begin from the back entrance of Liberty in **Argyll Street**, where the London Palladium is to be found, quite a large theatre by London standards. A traditional palace of varieties, it is the home of the annual Royal Variety Performance. **Great Marlborough Street**, round the corner, has the magistrates' court, which has also provided a variety of West End entertainment through the years. In fact, a one-time magistrate here was Edward Robey, son of the music hall comedian George Robey. Joan Lock, in her book *Marlborough Street*, tells us that a snake charmer in court for causing an obstruction was insulted when it was suggested that his snake was artificial. To prove his point the defendant pulled from his underpants a North American king snake over a metre long and the female court usher fled from the room in a panic.

The area around here is now pedestrianised, including **Carnaby Street**, still swinging since the sixties, or trying to, with interesting shops and cafes. **Berwick Street**, running north to south, is the home of London's most central street market, famed for fruit and veg. Parallel to it, **Wardour Street** has been described as the only street in London 'shady on both sides'.

MARX TIME?

David Benedictus knows London well, as his book, *Streets of London*, shows. He tells the story that at Leoni's Quo Vadis restaurant in **Dean Street**, Jascha Heifetz, the great violinist, needed a pianist to accompany him at a charity concert. Einstein readily agreed, but during the performance came in too late after the cadenza. 'What's the matter with you?' muttered Heifetz, 'Can't you count?' This restaurant, at 26 Dean Street, was the home of Karl Marx when he arrived in London. Canaletto lived in Soho during his stay in London, while others with connections were William Blake, Charles Lamb, Gainsborough, John Logie Baird and Dorothy L. Sayers.

DISMAL JIMMIE WINS AND LOSES

The area was rich hunting ground – Soho originally being a hunting cry – and was the home of the Duke of Monmouth, the oldest of Charles II's illegitimate sons. Charles's brother James inherited the throne in 1685 – 'Dismal Jimmie' as Nell Gwyn called him. He thought he could combine personal Catholicism with publicly defending the Protestant faith as king. The Protestant Monmouth thought *he* should be king and the dispute came to blows at Sedgemoor. Monmouth lost. Three years later Dismal Jimmie's Protestant daughter Mary and her husband William of Orange (both grandchildren of Charles I) stepped in and took over when James's rule came apart at the seams.

The area was colonised over the centuries by incomers: Huguenots, Chinese, Jews – Jack Solomons' gym was in **Great Windmill Street** – all with trades and services to offer. **Frith Street** is still the home of jazz, and here is Ronnie Scott's. Moving down to **Old Compton Street** – this is the area to buy breakfast, croissants and coffee at Patisserie Valerie, a fishy lunch at Wheeler's, and a pre-theatre drink at the French House – headquarters of the Free French during the war. The Chinese moved in south of **Shaftesbury Avenue** around **Gerrard Street** and **Lisle Street** where the lion dances at the Chinese New Year.

SHAFTESBURY AVENUE

Moving well into theatreland, here are the Lyric, Apollo, Globe, Queen's, Palace and (higher up) Shaftesbury. The Globe was built in the flush of London theatre building at the turn of the century and was originally called the Hicks after Seymour Hicks, the actor-manager who had a leading hand in its commissioning. When the Shakespearian Globe theatre has been reconstructed on the South Bank, opposite St Paul's, will the Edwardian Globe have to rename itself again?

The Palace, presently a sell out for 'Les Misérables', began life as Richard D'Oyly Carte's Royal English Opera House in 1891 with 'Ivanhoe' by Arthur Sullivan. The venture failed instantly and the theatre became the Palace Theatre of Varieties in 1892. The Palace still impresses from its imposing position at Cambridge Circus.

CHARING CROSS ROAD

Charing Cross Road is the place to buy books of all descriptions. Foyle's is the largest bookshop, but not necessarily the place to find the book you want. Waterstone's (at 121) will find out-of-print books, or try the Silver Moon for women's books, or Murder One in **Denmark Street** for classic first- and second-hand crime.

Across the road from Foyle's the Phoenix opened with Noel Coward and Gertrude Lawrence in 'Private Lives'. The theatre was to be the venue of several Coward productions. Always called 'The Master' in the profession, Coward once wrote to Winston Churchill inviting him to a first night: 'and bring a friend, if you have one'. Churchill replied that he was otherwise engaged for the first night, but would come to the second: 'if you have one'.

Further down the road, at the National Portrait Gallery end, the Garrick was built by W.S. Gilbert in the 1880s, though not without some difficulty as an underground river started to seep into the foundations. The exasperated Gilbert remarked with characteristic wit that he couldn't decide whether to continue with the building or to lease the fishing rights.

Clubs and discos

Bill Stickers, 18 Greek Street, W1
071-437 0582
Gossips, 69 Dean Street, W1
071-434 4480
100 Jazz Club, 100 Oxford Street, W1
071-636 0933
Marquee, 105 Charing Cross Road, WC2
071-437 6601/2/3
Moonlighting, 16 Greek Street, W1
071-734 6308
Ronnie Scott's, 47 Frith Street, W1
071-439 0747

Theatres

Apollo, Shaftesbury Avenue, W1
071-437 2663
Globe, Shaftesbury Avenue, W1
071-437 3667
London Palladium, Argyll Street, W1
071-437 7373
Lyric, Shaftesbury Avenue, W1
071-437 3686
Palace, Shaftesbury Avenue, W1
071-434 0909 (Les Misérables)
Piccadilly, Denman Street, W1
071-867 1118 (Rocky Horror Show)
Prince Edward, Old Compton Street, W1
071-734 8951
Queen's, Shaftesbury Avenue, W1
071-734 1166

Eating and drinking

(£ = up to £5 for one, ££ = up to £15 for one, £££ = up
to £25 for one, ££££ = the very special places)

Canton, 11 Newport Street, WC2
071-437 6220 (all-night Chinese cafe), £
Dragon Inn, 12 Gerrard Street, W1
071-494 0870, £££
Ed's Easy Diner, 12 Moor Street, W1
071-439 1955, £

The French House, 49 Dean Street, W1
071-437 2799, *££-£££*
The Gay Hussar, 2 Greek Street, W1
071-437 0973 (Hungarian), *£££-££££*
Harry's, 19 Kingly Street, W1
071-434 0309, open Mon-Fri 10 pm-9 am, Sat until 6 am
(all-night breakfasts), *£*
Leoni's Quo Vadis Restaurant, 26 Dean Street, W1
071-437 9585, *££££*
Maharani, 77 Berwick Street, W1
071-437 8568 (Indian), *££*
Patisserie Valerie, 44 Old Compton Street, W1
071-437 3466, *£*
Pizza Express, 10 Dean Street, W1
071-437 9595 (admission charge for live jazz), *££*
Wheeler's, 19-21 Old Compton Street, W1
071-437 2706 (fish), *£££*

COVENT GARDEN

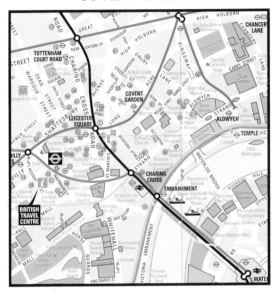

Covent Garden and the spread outwards of small shops, craft workshops and places to eat and drink have made this area a mecca for visitors from **Charing Cross Road** in the west to **Drury Lane** in the east. The New London theatre, near the top end of Drury Lane, is a theatre of the new age with stage, seats, lights and even walls that can change position to suit the individual show. In fact, for 'Cats' a notice says: 'Latecomers not admitted while auditorium is in motion' – take travel pills! The Royal Opera House in **Bow Street** opened in 1732, the second theatre to be licensed to perform drama (the Theatre Royal, Drury Lane was the first). It burned down in 1808, as did its successor in 1856.

Royal Opera House

The present building dates from 1858. Originally an opera house concentrating on Italian opera, it widened its scope when Sir Thomas Beecham brought over Diaghilev's Russian ballet.

GHOSTS OF OLD DRURY

The Theatre Royal, Drury Lane, is full of ghosts. One story used to be told of a knight in armour wandering about backstage when there was no one in that costume in the current play. Was it here that Grimaldi, the clown, hanged himself from the rafters high above the stage? The famous ghost is the Man in Grey, dressed in fashionable clothes and wig of the 1750s, who is seen – never later than 6 pm – in the upper circle.

The present building is the fourth on the site since 1662 when the King's Company of Players were in residence after the restoration of the monarchy. It was here that Nell Gwyn caught both His Majesty's eye and his ear. Hers was one of the few voices to rise above the rabble as she traded (in oranges, naturally) in the stalls. Her ready wit and obvious charms got her where she wanted to be, but only to the age of 37, when she died after a short illness, to be buried at St Martin-in-the-Fields. Garrick was manager at Drury Lane in the eighteenth century. He came down from Lichfield with Samuel Johnson in 1737, both of them to make their fortunes in the capital.

Covent Garden

SMALL IS BEAUTIFUL

Endell Street Place (27-29 **Endell Street**) has a glass-roofed gallery and craftspeople woodcarving, spinning and potting. Glassblowing can be seen in the Glasshouse in **Long Acre**. Neal's Yard, off **Neal Street**, has similar small businesses and health foods, while Neal Street has Mary Quant and the tiny Hat Shop, where customers have to queue in the street.

For the body beautiful see the Sport section for details of Pineapple in **Langley Street**, the Oasis in **Endell Street** and the Sanctuary in **Floral Street**. Recover from a session at Pineapple with a Mexican meal at the Cafe Pacifico next door, or vice versa.

St Paul's, Covent Garden

Russell Street has the Fortune theatre, the Theatre Museum and Boswell's coffee shop, where James Boswell met Dr Johnson in 1762, though it was a bookshop then. The Old Flower Market houses the London Transport Museum in the far corner, and moving to the Central Hall, a

London Transport Museum

board gives the locations of the shopkeepers and cafes in the central covered market. St Paul's, the actors' church, at the far end, has a quiet garden away from the bustle of the piazza and Punch and Judy shows from time to time. See Events month by month for details. All in all the whole area provides entertainment almost all round the clock.

CHIC AND CHEERFUL

To eat and drink in the area north of the piazza, Peter Stringfellow has Stringfellow's, 16-19 **Upper St Martin's**

Lane, art deco disco and restaurant till the early hours, and the Hippodrome, near **Leicester Square** tube station where admittance is idiosyncratic (says *Time Out*). Or try the theatrical restaurant, the Ivy, in **West Street**, refurbished in glamorous style by Chris Corbin and Jeremy King of Le Caprice. Here also are the Ambassadors and St Martin's theatres, which between them have hosted 'The Mousetrap' since 25 November 1952. Both theatres are quite small, seating around 500 each, a perfect intimate atmosphere to eavesdrop on the English 'cozy' from the Queen of Crime.

The Lamb & Flag is quite close at 33 **Rose Street**, off Floral Street. This timbered building of boisterous fame was once nick-named the 'Bucket of Blood' when bare fist fights were held up-stairs. Here the poet Dryden was roughed over for writing insulting verses.

London Coliseum

PETER PAN

Moving down **St Martin's Lane**, the Duke of York's theatre was where 'Peter Pan' opened in 1904, to be revived here every Christmas to 1915. And here too is the London Coliseum, home of English National Opera since the former Sadler's Wells Opera made it their West End home. The ball on top was meant to revolve, but now it is still. The theatre was built in 1904 by Oswald Stoll with a furnished lift, or mobile lounge, designed to transport royal guests in comfort and privacy to their box.

RULES RULES

Sometimes, with refurbishments and rebuildings, a sense of permanence that should be associated with long-established eating houses is lost. But down towards the

Strand find Rules at 35 **Maiden Lane** (behind the Adelphi theatre) and Simpson's in the Strand, which have remained through two world wars and more. Booking and correct dress are essential.

ACT OF MURDER

In the days when the music hall song went 'Let's all go down the Strand', the Adelphi, Vaudeville and the long gone Gaiety were the bright lights that Londoners headed for. One December evening in 1897 the popular Victorian actor William Terriss was stabbed to death outside the Adelphi theatre, where he had a starring role, by out-of-work actor Richard Prince. The successful Terriss had earlier that day given Prince a handout, which the resentful actor used to buy the dagger that killed his benefactor shortly before curtain up. Terriss's ghost hovers

about the theatre still and sometimes knocks on the leading lady's dressing room door before a performance. Terriss used to eat at Rules, according to Jonathan Goodman, who tells the story of his death in *Acts of Murder.*

Savoy theatre

VAUDEVILLE DAYS

The smaller Vaudeville theatre is a delight. I saw Dame Sybil Thorndike and Athene Seyler here in a weekday matinee of 'Arsenic and Old Lace' twenty-five years ago. There were only a few people in the audience and tea in china cups was brought round to the seats in the interval. The poor attendance had no effect, of course, on the performances of two great ladies of the stage.

The Savoy, next to the Savoy Hotel, was the home of the D'Oyly Carte company who performed Gilbert and Sullivan's comic operas, such a feature of late Victorian life. Built in 1881, this was the first theatre to have electric lights installed.

Clubs and discos

Laceys, 81 St Martin's Lane, WC2
071-240 8187
Stringfellow's, 16 Upper St Martin's Lane, WC2
071-240 5534
Sunday Night at Freud's, 198 Shaftesbury Avenue, WC2
071-240 9933

Theatres

Adelphi, Strand, WC2
071-836 7611 (Me and My Girl)
Albery, St Martin's Lane, WC2
071-867 1115 (Blood Brothers)
Aldwych, Aldwych, WC2
071-836 6404
Ambassadors, West Street, WC2
071-836 6111
Arts, Cranbourn Street, WC2
071-836 2132
Cambridge, Earlham Street, WC2
071-379 5299 (Return to the Forbidden Planet)
Dominion, Tottenham Court Road, W1
071-580 9562 (42nd Street)
Duchess, Catherine Street, WC2
071-836 8243
Duke of York's, St Martin's Lane, WC2
071-836 5122 (Shirley Valentine)
Fortune, Russell Street, WC2
071-836 2238 (The Woman in Black)
Garrick, Charing Cross Road, WC2
071-379 6107
London Coliseum, St Martin's Lane, WC2
071-836 3161
New London, Drury Lane, WC2
071-405 0072 (Cats)
Phoenix, Charing Cross Road, WC2
071-867 1044
Playhouse, Northumberland Avenue, WC2
071-839 4401
Royal Opera House, Covent Garden, WC2
071-240 1066/1911
St Martin's, West Street, WC2
071-836 1443 (The Mousetrap)

Savoy, Strand, WC2
071-836 8888
Shaftesbury, Shaftesbury Avenue, WC2
071-379 5399
Strand, Aldwych, WC2
071-240 0300
Theatre Royal, Drury Lane, WC2
071-379 4444/240 7200
Vaudeville, Strand, WC2
071-836 9987
Wyndhams, Charing Cross Road, WC2
071-867 1116

Eating and drinking

(£ = up to £5 for one, ££ = up to £15 for one, £££ = up
to £25 for one, ££££ = the very special places)
Café des Amis du Vin, 11-14 Hanover Place, WC2
071-379 3444, ££
Cafe Pacifico, 5 Langley Street, WC2
071-379 7728 (Mexican), ££
Dome Restaurant, 34 Wellington Street, WC2
071-836 0998 (cafe-bar), £
Green and Pleasant, 111 Long Acre, WC2
071-240 7781 (salads), £
The Ivy, 1-5 West Street, WC2
071-836 4751, £££
Lamb & Flag, 33 Rose Street, WC2
071-836 4108, £
Porters, 17 Henrietta Street, WC2
071-836 6466 (English pies), £-££
Rock and Sole Place, 47 Endell Street, WC2
071-836 3785 (fish and chips), £
Rock Garden, 6-7 The Piazza, WC2
071-240 3961, ££-£££
Rules Restaurant, 35 Maiden Lane, WC2
071-836 5314 (English fare – booking essential), £££
Simpson's in the Strand, 100 Strand, WC2
071-836 9112, ££

LEICESTER SQUARE

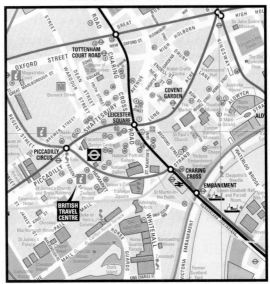

Our route round the West End has meandered in a roughly clockwise direction to conclude in the small area which has **Leicester Square** at its centre. Here, half-price tickets for the night's shows can be obtained from the booth of the Society of West End Theatres. Around you is the centre of West End cinema and theatre life, where once stood the Old Curiosity Shop that inspired Dickens. (The shop of that name near Lincoln's Inn Fields was a heraldic sign-painter's shop in Dickens' day.) To emphasise the square's debt to theatre and cinema, here are statues to the king of each – Shakespeare and Charlie Chaplin.

THEATRE IN THE HAY

To the south of the square is **Haymarket**. The Theatre Royal, Haymarket, was the third theatre in London to be licensed after the Restoration. The 'Little Theatre in the Hay' held illegal performances until it received the royal patent in the time of George III. It was restored by Beau Nash in 1821 and became the Theatre Royal.

Across the road the 'Phantom of the Opera' at Her Majesty's is likely to be sold out for several months ahead. The theatre started out as the King's theatre until 1837 when it was renamed in honour of the new Queen. The present theatre on the site was built by Beerbohm Tree in 1897.

At the bottom of Haymarket is the start of St James's with Pall Mall and the beginning of this amble, ramble – in case you started in the middle and wish to continue.

Clubs and discos
Café de Paris, 3 Coventry Street, WC1
071-437 2036
The Hippodrome, Charing Cross Road, WC2
071-437 4311

Theatres
Comedy, Panton Street, SW1
071-867 1045
Haymarket (Theatre Royal), Haymarket, SW1
071-930 8800
Her Majesty's, Haymarket, SW1
071-839 2244 (Phantom of the Opera)
Prince of Wales, Coventry Street, W1
071-839 5972 (Aspects of Love)

Eating and drinking
(£ = up to £5 for one, ££ = up to £15 for one, £££ = up to £25 for one, ££££ = the very special places)
Corner House, The Strand (opposite Charing Cross station), WC2
071-930 9381, £·££
Stockpot, 40 Panton Street, SW1
071-839 5142, ££

"THE GREATEST MUSICAL OF THE DECADE"

Sheridan Morley • Punch & International Herald Tribune

WILLY RUSSELL'S
AWARD WINNING MUSICAL

BLOOD
Brothers

"STANDS HEAD AND SHOULDERS ABOVE EVERY OTHER SHOW IN TOWN"

BBC Radio

ALBERY THEATRE
St. Martins Lane • WC2

BOX OFFICE & CREDIT CARDS: 071 867 111

LOOK INTO THE PAST

AT THE LONDON TRANSPORT MUSEUM

Browse among our unique collection of historic vehicles, posters and archive film.

Put yourself in the driving seat of a London bus or Underground train.

Visit the Museum Shop for the best selection of reproduction posters in town.

Open Daily 10.00-18.00. (Last admission 17.15). Museum closed 24/25/26 Dec. Phone 071-379 6344 071-836 8557 24 hr. information.

How to get there: *Underground:* Covent Garden or Leicester Square *British Rail:* Charing Cross. *Bus:* Any bus to Aldwych or Strand.

London Transport Museum, The Piazza, Covent Garden, London WC2E 7BB.

Posters

T-shirts

Books

Models

Gifts

Cards

Videos

Souvenirs

Games

Ever Changing

LONDON TRANSPORT MUSEUM SHOP PRESENTS LINES THAT GO ON AND ON

There are many gift shops in London, few, however, are as varied and interesting as ours. There's something for everyone from five to ninety-five. From Aberdeen to Zagreb, Paris to Pittsburg. Old ticket machines to highest quality English Crystal. Tube mugs, beautiful poster art books to transport magazines, children's toys and fine models. We present the best of London and its transport. With so much to offer it's no wonder we say our lines go on and on.

New Lines

London Transport Museum Shop.
Open 7 days a week 10.00 to 18.00.

The Piazza, Covent Garden, London WC2

LONDON TRANSPORT MUSEUM

Red buses have taken the place of red roses in the Old Flower Market on the south-east corner of Covent Garden Piazza. This beautiful Victorian building in which London's most famous flower seller, Eliza Doolittle, once bought her stock is now the setting for one of London's most unusual museums.

The London Transport Museum tells the story of the capital's public transport from the era of the horse bus to the present day. The museum is the home of London Transport's unique collection of historic vehicles, archive film and photography, memorabilia and graphic art.

The museum is a lively place to visit. There is a regular programme of exhibitions covering a wide range of topics. From time to time special events are arranged, from children's competitions to collectors' markets. The working displays and interactive exhibits are especially popular with younger visitors.

The story of London's buses began when George Shillibeer introduced his omnibus service in 1829. Fares were far from cheap (6d and 1s) but the idea caught on and within thirty years there were over eight hundred horse buses operating in London. A replica of Shillibeer's beautiful omnibus and a restored 'knife board' horse bus

The original padded cell – an exhibit from the Tube Centenary

are on display at the museum.

By 1910 petrol buses had become a practical proposition and the museum's collection includes one of the famous 'B' type buses introduced in that year. The more modern buses are an invitation to wallow in nostalgia – the Green Line coach, an ST bus that survived the Blitz and a stately trolleybus that purred along London's streets in the late 1930s are all reminders of London's recent past. Visitors can even put themselves in the driver's seat of a modern double-decker, try the controls and imagine how it would feel to negotiate London's traffic in such a huge vehicle.

Londoners have travelled by Underground railway since the 1860s. The first Underground

Buses and trams on display in the Museum.

lines used steam and the museum has a beautiful 1866 Metropolitan Line locomotive on display. The story of Underground electric railways is told by Tube Centenary, a major exhibition set in a replica Victorian tube station. Actor guides and working models bring the story of the tube to life. A full-size mock-up of the new generation of Central Line train and a simulator that allows visitors to 'drive' one of the new trains give a glimpse of the future.

London Transport has always demanded high standards of design for everything from bus stops to its celebrated posters. The Frank Pick Gallery – named after London Transport's famous Chief Executive of the 1930s – is dedicated to exhibitions on all aspects of art and design. Around three different topics are covered each year and the gallery is always worth a browse.

Families with children are made welcome at the museum. Children under 5 years of age are admitted free of charge and it is easy to get a pram to any part of the museum. A parents' room for feeding and changing babies is available. Disabled visitors (who are admitted free of charge) will also find the museum accessible and there are special toilet facilities for wheelchair users.

If you want an Underground map tee shirt, a reproduction station clock for the hall or even a bus conductor's ticket machine, the museum shop is well worth a visit. The shop stocks a wide range of souvenirs and gifts – many exclusive to the museum. It also carries the best selection of reproduction posters in town and a range of postcards to delight collectors.

The London Transport Museum is open every day of the year (except 24-26 December) from 10 to 6. Last admissions are at 5.15. There is a charge for admission but there are concessions for children, students, senior citizens and the unemployed. Families with children can buy special family tickets which admit two adults and two children at a bargain price.

ENTERTAINMENT FURTHER AFIELD

Clubs and discos

Camden Palace, 1 Camden Road, NW1
071-387 0428
Dingwalls, Camden Lock, Chalk Farm Road, NW1
071-267 4967
Electric Ballroom, 184 Camden High Street, NW1
071-485 9006

Theatres and concert halls

Apollo Victoria, Wilton Road, SW1
071-828 8665 (Starlight Express)
Barbican Centre, Silk Street, EC2
071-638 8891(Concerts, plays, exhibitions, major
festivals, films – The Royal Shakespeare Company may be
seen at the Barbican)
Lyric Theatre Hammersmith, King Street, W6
081-741 2311
National Theatre, South Bank, SE1
071-928 2252
The New Shakespeare Co. Ltd, The Open Air Theatre,
Regent's Park, NW1
071-935 5756/5884 (open-air Shakespeare in the
summer; see also Parks section)
Old Vic, Waterloo Road, SE1
071-928 7616
Royal Albert Hall, Kensington Gore, SW7
071-589 3203
South Bank Centre, SE1
071-921 0600 (Royal Festival Hall, Queen Elizabeth Hall
and Purcell Room. Nearby are Hayward Gallery, National
Film Theatre, National Theatre and Museum of the
Moving Image)
Whitehall, Whitehall, SW1
071-867 1119 (Absurd Person Singular)
Victoria Palace, Victoria Street, SW1
071-834 1317 (Buddy)

Eating

(£ = up to £5 for one, ££ = up to £15 for one, £££ = up to £25 for one, ££££ = the very special places)

Café Rouge, Hampstead High Street, NW3
071-433 3404, ££-£££

Chelsea Kitchen, 98 King's Road, SW3
071-489 1330, ££

Daquise, 20 Thurloe Street, South Kensington, SW7
071-589 6117, £-££

Indian Veg, 92 Chapel Market, Islington, N1
071-837 4607, booking essential, £-££

Ken Lo's Memories of China, 67-69 Ebury Street, SW1
071-730 7734/4276, ££££

Michel's, 6 Holland Street, W8
071-937 3367 (traditional French), ££

Pasta Prego, 1a Beauchamp Place, SW1
071-225 1064, £-££

Primrose Patisserie, 136 Regent's Park Road, Primrose Hill, NW1
071-722 7848, £

Thames-side inns

The Anchor Bankside, 34 Park Street, SE1
071-407 1577

Dickens Pub, St Katharine's Way, E1
071-488 2208/9932

The Doggetts Coat and Badge, 1 Blackfriars Bridge, SE1
071-633 9081

Prospect of Whitby, 57 Wapping Wall, E1
071-481 1095

Town of Ramsgate, 62 Wapping High Street, E1
071-488 2685

Royal National Theatre

~~Gallery~~

~~River Terraces~~

~~Bookshop~~

~~Backstage Tours~~

~~Restaurant~~

~~Live Music~~

~~Cafe~~

Some theatre.

The Royal National Theatre is a great place to take a break - there's so much to choose from, like foyer concerts and exhibitions, or our theatre Bookshop. We also give backstage tours every day except Sunday, a unique experience at a price everyone can afford.

We have three theatres offering a great choice, from dazzling comedies to classic tragedies. Special discounts are available for groups of 12 or more, and there are lower price matinees too. Each day we hold back some tickets for sale from 10am, so there's a chance of catching even our most popular productions if you come early.

Some of the best views of London can be seen from our riverside terraces, and there are bars, cafés and a restaurant serving realistically priced refreshments. So put a trip to the National on your itinerary and phone 071-633 0880 to find out more.

ROYAL NATIONAL THEATRE,
SOUTH BANK, LONDON SE1 9PX
⊖ WATERLOO OR
EMBANKMENT, ⇌ WATERLOO
FOYERS OPEN 10AM - 11PM
MONDAY-SATURDAY.

ROYAL
NATIONAL
THEATRE

EVENTS MONTH BY MONTH

The London Tourist Board (LTB) publishes a list of traditional events each January to help you plan your trip to the capital. Phone LTB on 071-730 3488 for exact dates. For events in the City call in or phone the information bureau in St Paul's Churchyard on 071-606 3030. Acknowledgements to LTB for supplying the information below. Note that all guidebooks are out of date in some respects by the time they appear, so do check with the relevant tourist body before setting out.

DAILY

The Horse Guards leave their barracks in Hyde Park at 10.28 am Mondays to Saturdays, 9.28 on Sundays, for the ceremony at Horse Guards, Whitehall, at 11 am, 10 am

Horse Guards

on Sundays. Henry VIII held Court at Whitehall Palace, which was the royal palace until it burned down in 1698 (with the exception of the Banqueting House). William III moved the Court to St James's Palace but Horse Guards is still regarded as the official entrance to the royal palaces. **Changing the guard** at Buckingham Palace every day is at 11.30 daily from April to the end of July and on alternate days from August to approximately the end of March.

Guard changing ceremonies also take place at Windsor Castle and the Tower.

NIGHTLY

Whatever time of year you plan to be in London, with advance planning it should be possible to attend the nightly **Ceremony of the Keys** at the Tower. Write to the Governor, Tower of London, EC3N 4AB, with as many alternative dates as possible. The locking-up ceremony takes seven minutes as the Chief Yeoman Warder, carrying a lantern in one hand and the Queen's Keys in the other, tours the gates of the Tower with an escort. He is challenged with the time-honoured phrase: 'Halt! Who goes there?' and answers 'The Keys' at each gate until he delivers the keys to the Queen's House and the guard is dismissed. But how do the visitors get out?

JANUARY

New Year's Day is the day when coachloads of hardy annuals arrive at the Serpentine in tracksuits, strip off and leap into the water, watched from the icy shore by three joggers and a suspicious doberman. On Twelfth Night, 6 January, officers of the royal household offer up gifts of gold, frankincense and myrrh at the **Royal Epiphany Gifts Service**, Chapel Royal, St James's Palace, SW1. Charles I prayed here before losing his head outside the Banqueting House in Whitehall.

His execution is remembered on the last Sunday in January by the King's Army, the Royalist Wing of the English Civil War Society, who assemble in authentic dress outside St James's Palace at 11 am. They follow Charles' route to the scaffold through Horse Guards to lay a wreath at the Banqueting House before returning via the statue of the King in Trafalgar Square and the Mall at 12.45.

FEBRUARY

The **Chinese New Year** occurs at different dates depending on the cycles of the moon. On the nearest Sunday Soho goes completely Chinese with the new year festival and lion dances in the streets. In 1992 the Chinese New Year is on 4 February for the Year of the Monkey. Celebrations take place on 9 February.

The Queen came to the throne on 6 February 1952, and on the anniversary of her accession a **41-gun salute** is fired at noon in Hyde Park followed by a 62-gun salute at the Tower of London at 1 pm. (If 6 February is a Sunday the guns are fired on the following day.)

MARCH

On a blustery Saturday before Easter the annual **Oxford and Cambridge** boat race is held over 4¼ miles between

Putney Bridge and Mortlake. This has been an annual event since 1856 and attracts less and less attention from the media unless the cox is a photogenic girl or someone sinks.

If you visit Fleet Street on the second Tuesday in March, be at St Bride's church, at the bottom of the street, at noon to see the Lord Mayor of London attend a service in dedication and thanksgiving for the founding of Bridewell Royal Hospital in the former Bridewell Palace by Edward VI. Part

St Bride's

of this became the notorious Bridewell House of Correction, closed in 1863, and part evolved into the present King Edward VI's School in Witley, Surrey. (The word 'hospital' did not imply a house for the sick in the Middle Ages, but for strangers.)

The church of St Clement Danes in the Strand rings out the old nursery rhyme 'Oranges and Lemons' daily at 9, 12, 3 and 6, and welcomes the children of St Clement Danes Primary School on the third or fourth Thursday in March for the 3 o'clock **Oranges and Lemons Service** beginning with the peal. Afterwards each child is given an orange and a lemon.

The advent of official spring brings out the Druids, who gather to celebrate the equinox on 21 March or thereabouts on Tower Hill at noon with a seed planting ceremony.

EASTER

The morning service on Good Friday at St Bartholomew-the-Great, Smithfield, is concluded by the distribution of money and hot cross buns. This custom, the **Butterworth Charity**, originated from a will leaving twenty-one sixpences on a grave in the churchyard for poor widows. Any service at this ancient church is worth attending. It was founded by the monk Rahere in 1123, who also

St Clement Danes

founded St Bartholomew's Hospital. His tomb is in the church, which is reached via a half-timbered gate-house. The church is a gem, a miraculous survival of the Great Fire of London and the Luftwaffe.

Battersea Park is the venue for the **Easter Parade**, which progresses round the perimeter with bonnets, Easter Princess competition, floats and jazz band in the afternoon of Easter Sunday.

Easter Monday sees the **Harness Horse Parade** in Regent's Park on the Inner Circle (**U** Baker Street).

These are working horses, and the show is free, beginning in the morning.

APRIL

The first Thursday after Easter at noon gives an opportunity to see the fine livery of the Lord Mayor, sheriffs and aldermen of the City of London as they go in procession across the yard from Guildhall to the church of St Lawrence Jewry-next-Guildhall. Here is preached the **Spital Sermon**, a tradition dating back to the Middle Ages though the site has changed. It was originally given at an outdoor pulpit on the site of the Hospital of St Mary Spital, founded in 1197.

Another church service takes place in April at St

Andrew Undershaft, Leadenhall Street, EC3, to remember **John Stow** (1525-1605), the London historian who ended life as a beggar because writing history didn't pay. A statue of Stow shows him with a quill in his hand, replaced each year, when an address is given by a notable historian. As I went by the church in September 1990 the doors were shut and construction work was going on all about me. Its churches are the City's only links with the past. They don't deserve to be jostled and loomed over by plate glass. I plan to go to this service myself if it survives.

Another **gun salute** takes place on the Queen's birthday on 21 April, unless it falls on a Sunday, when it takes place on the Monday following. See February for details.

Among the thousands hanged at Tyburn, where Marble Arch stands, were many persecuted Catholics. These are remembered on the last Sunday in April in the **Tyburn Walk**, a silent afternoon procession led by a Catholic bishop along the old route from Newgate Gaol (Old Bailey) to Tyburn Convent (8 Hyde Park Place, W2, off the Bayswater Road near Marble Arch).

MAY

Make an early start on the first Sunday in May to see the London to Brighton **Historic Commercial Vehicle Run**, from 6.30 am onwards in Crystal Palace Park – buses, fire engines, delivery vans and military vehicles. The run is part of the Wheels of Yesterday Rally which starts on the Saturday.

The first Wednesday in May sees the **Derby** race at Epsom, the major flat racing event of the year.

Members of the public are welcome to attend the **Dunkirk Veterans' Service** at 3 o'clock on a Sunday in May at the church of St Lawrence Jewry-next-Guildhall, EC2. Veterans march from Swan Court to the church and wreaths are laid afterwards.

The City boasts many ancient traditions but a more recent one that combines fun with function is the **target spraying competition** by the London Private Fire Brigades in Guildhall Yard. Spectators are welcome to watch teams compete for the Silver Challenge Shield presented by the Corporation of the City of London.

Teams are not allowed to spray spectators, or each other! Phone the City information line, 071-606 3030, for details of the competition held at noon on a Saturday in May and September.

May and September also see **Punch and Judy Festivals** in Covent Garden. Pepys watched Punch and Judy here at St Paul's church on 9 May 1662 and to commemorate this, usually on the second Sunday in May, a procession round Covent Garden takes place followed by an 11 o'clock service in the church. Punch and Judy shows are held in the church garden. Inquire at the Actor's Church Union office in the church.

Ascension Day – the sixth Thursday after Easter – is marked in two London parishes by the ceremony of **beating the bounds**, which anyone can watch. Every three years at about 6 o'clock on Ascension Day evening a colourful procession starts from the Tower chapel of St Peter ad Vincula when the Chief Yeoman Warder in his red uniform leads the choirboys round thirty-one parish boundary marks in surrounding streets. The traffic is stopped where necessary so that the chaplain may recite a prayer and the choirboys literally beat the mark with willow wands.

The nearest City church to the Tower, All Hallows-by-the-Tower, has an annual Ascension Day beating the bounds ceremony at 3 pm. The public can join but as one of the marks is in mid-Thames visitors have to watch from the shore as the official party goes to the middle of the river

All Hallows-by-the-Tower

by boat. Here an unfortunate boy – or perhaps it's a great honour – is hung over the side by the ankles as he beats the boundary on the side of the boat. When the two processions meet, every three years on Tower Hill, a ceremonial challenge between the City and the Tower takes place on this historically disputed mark.

Chelsea Flower Show begins in late May run by the Royal Horticultural Society in the gardens of the Royal Hospital, Chelsea. Phone the RHS headquarters in Vincent Square on 071-828 1744 for recorded details of this and other seasonal shows.

JUNE

The main event of the year without a doubt is **Trooping the Colour,** held on the second Sunday in June to celebrate the Queen's official birthday. Its original function was to display the regimental flag to the men so they would recognise it on the battlefield. The Queen, escorted by the Household Cavalry, leaves Buckingham Palace down the Mall to arrive at Horse Guards at 11 am. She returns to the palace at 12.30 for a flypast by the RAF at 1 o'clock. Tickets are much sought after and allocated by ballot, two per application. Write before the end of

Windsor

February to the Brigade Major (Trooping the Colour), Headquarters, Household Division, Horse Guards, SW1A 2AX. The birthday **gun salute** to the Queen is held at 11 am in Green Park and at 1 pm at the Tower.

If you want to hedge your bets, **Beating Retreat** and **Sounding Retreat** are spectacular ceremonies (without the Queen) on Horse Guards Parade in June. The 'retreat' is not from battle, but from daylight. Some performances are floodlit. Tickets from the end of February from Premier Box Office, 1b Bridge Street, SW1, 071-839 6815/071-836 4114.

Her Majesty goes down to Windsor during the third week in June for **Royal Ascot** and the royal party go in procession in open carriages down the course before the start of racing. Thursday – Ladies' Day – is the day when amazing hats are worn. Tickets from the Secretary, Grandstand, Ascot, Berks.

The **Garter Service** at St George's Chapel, Windsor, is also held in June but is not open to the public. The Royal Order of the Garter is the highest of the ancient orders of chivalry, reserved for members of the Royal Family, foreign royalty and statesmen. The ceremony, attended by the knights, is for the investiture of any new knights. Al-

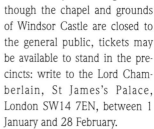

though the chapel and grounds of Windsor Castle are closed to the general public, tickets may be available to stand in the precincts: write to the Lord Chamberlain, St James's Palace, London SW14 7EN, between 1 January and 28 February.

Prince Philip is also accorded a **gun salute** on his birthday, 10 June. See February for details.

Pepys is remembered some time in June with a **Pepys Commemoration Service** in St Olave's church, Hart Street, EC3 (across the busy road from the Tower and up Seething Lane) where Pepys and his wife were buried. Write to the church for

details of the service and the buffet lunch.

A midsummer ceremony in the City is held at Guild-hall (apply in advance for tickets to the Keeper, Guildhall, EC2P 2EJ) when the two sheriffs of the City are elected. This office dates back to the seventh century. The sheriffs attend the Lord Mayor at official functions and are present

St Olave's church

every day at the Central Criminal Court (Old Bailey), which is within the City.

JULY

The **Royal Tournament** is a spectacular show presented by the armed forces at Earl's Court in mid-July to demonstrate their skill. The Queen and other senior members of the Royal Family take the salute. This is one of the major shows of the capital and if you are unable to get tickets it is usually on television. Write from mid-March to Royal Tournament Box Office, Earl's Court Exhibition Centre, Warwick Road, SW5 9TA.

AUGUST

The Queen Mother's birthday on 4 August is remembered by a **gun salute** on this day. See February for details.

Guildhall Yard is the scene of an intriguing ceremony each year, usually held in August, at midday, when the **Cart Marking Ceremony** takes place. Originally this involved branding a registration number and the City's coat of arms on a vehicle with a hot iron. It dates from 1681 when the number of carts plying their trade in the City was limited to 421. Now the branding – done by the Keeper of Guildhall – takes the form of a metal plate. Could this have been the origin of the numberplate?

Rotten Row is still used by equestrians today as it was when it was opened by William III in 1690. The best time to see riders – or join them – is during the **London Riding Horse Parade** on the first Sunday in August. There are several classes of entry for the best turned-out horse and rider. Phone LTB for the address of the current secretary of the parade for an entry form and details.

Royal Tournament

August Bank Holiday – the last Monday in August – and the Sunday before it are the dates of the Notting Hill Carnival, a popular West Indian event around the streets of Notting Hill and Ladbroke Grove.

SEPTEMBER

The Druid Order hold **autumn equinox** celebrations at Primrose Hill, above Regent's Park, at the equinox when fruits are scattered on the ground carrying seeds for the coming spring.

Henry Fitz Aylwyn was the first Mayor of London in 1192 and the unbroken tradition continues with the annual election of the Lord Mayor (as the office is called today) at Michaelmas, on or near 29 September. The election ceremony, known as **Common Hall**, takes place in Guildhall at midday after a procession of the Lord Mayor and sheriffs from Mansion House, the official residence of the Lord Mayor. Tickets are available from the Keeper, Guildhall. A public church service is held beforehand at St Lawrence Jewry, close by, attended by the Lord Mayor, aldermen and robed masters of all the City livery companies. This has been a tradition since the election of Richard Whittington as Mayor in 1406.

On the last Sunday in September or first in October the **Punch and Judy Fellowship** holds a festival of Punch and Judy shows in Covent Garden throughout the day.

OCTOBER

Although some of London's most colourful events are private, they are often accompanied by a procession through the streets which visitors may be lucky enough to catch. On the first weekday in October, at the beginning of the legal year, there is a service for judges in Westminster Abbey dating back to the Middle Ages, followed by a breakfast in the Royal Gallery of the Houses of Parliament. Their Lordships may be spotted in solemn tread stepping across from the abbey to the Houses of Parliament at 11.45 am.

The first Pearly King was Henry Croft, a cockney costermonger (street trader) who lived around 1880 and who sewed pearl buttons on his clothes. He started collecting for charity and after his death the tradition continued. The Pearly Kings and Queens can be seen centrally at the church of St Martin-in-the-Fields, Trafalgar Square, in the **Pearly Harvest Festival** at 3 pm on the first Sunday in October.

Pepys' church – St Olave's, Hart Street – is also the parish church of the wine and spirit trade of London and on the first Tuesday in October at midday is the scene of the **Vintage Festival Service**. The masters and wardens of the Worshipful Company of Vintners and Distillers attend in full regalia to celebrate the year's wine harvest. Check details on 071-606 3030 or with the church.

A fishy service is normally held at the church of St Mary-at-Hill, Eastcheap, EC3 (near the Monument) on the second Sunday in October in thanksgiving for the **Harvest of the Sea**, as this is the church of Billingsgate Fish Market, formerly nearby. (The service is temporarily at St Margaret Pattens, Rood Lane.) A variety of fish is displayed in the vestibule and the morning service is attended by the aldermen and Common Council of the Ward, who come in state. The Court of Common Council's meetings at Guildhall are open to the public every third Thursday at 1 pm. They have been meeting since the twelfth century. The City information bureau has details on 071-606 3030.

Trafalgar Day, 21 October, is the anniversary of the great sea battle that saw the death of Nelson. On the Wednesday nearest this date a **Service for Seafarers** is held at St Paul's Cathedral, Nelson's burial place, at 6 pm, accompanied by the band of the Royal Marines. Tickets are obtainable from the Hon. Sec. of the Annual National Service for Seafarers, St Michael Paternoster Royal, College Hill, EC4R 2RL. This simple church was also Richard Whittington's parish church and although the great benefactor's tomb was destroyed in the war, an attractive modern stained-glass window shows him with his cat.

NOVEMBER

Guy Fawkes and his fellow conspirators intended their fireworks display to coincide with the **State Opening of Parliament**. They were discovered without having lit the blue touchpaper by the Yeomen of the Guard. The Houses of Parliament did burn down in the nineteenth century, by accident, and the buildings you see from the street or river today are the results of a competition won by (Sir) Charles Barry (presumably the knighthood was for his achievement). Yeomen of the Guard still check the cellars annually prior to the State Opening of Parliament in early to mid-November and all around the country bonfires and firework displays are held on or near 5 November. Phone LTB for details of public displays in London from October onwards. The most central is likely to be on Primrose Hill, 7-8 pm.

The State Opening of Parliament by the Queen is not open to the public but is usually on television. People line the streets to watch the procession leave Buckingham Palace at approximately 11 am. The Queen and Prince Philip travel in the Irish State Coach, which can otherwise be visited in the Royal Mews (phone 071-799 2331 for recorded opening times).

The London to Brighton **Veteran Car Run** takes place on the first Sunday in November starting from Hyde Park Corner between 8 and 9 in the morning. It began in 1896 when the law compelling motorists to drive behind a man carrying a red flag was abolished. Only cars made before 1905 can take part.

The gilded coach in the Museum of London is on duty in the streets on the second Saturday of November for the **Lord Mayor's Show**. The new Lord Mayor travels to the

Royal Courts of Justice to swear allegiance to the Sovereign, represented by the justices, surrounded by his personal bodyguard of the Company of Pikemen and Musketeers. Colourful floats and bands from the uniformed services make up the procession, which starts at 11 am. It is on the day before this splendid – and noisy – show, on the Friday, that the new Lord Mayor takes office and changes place in total silence with the outgoing Mayor. Tickets from the Keeper of Guildhall.

On the second Sunday in November members of the armed forces and ex-service personnel assemble at the Cenotaph in Whitehall to remember the dead of two

world wars. The two-minute silence at 11 am is followed by the Last Post and the Queen lays a wreath on the Cenotaph, followed by members of the Royal Family and representatives of the government, Commonwealth governments and the services.

DECEMBER

In 1343, even before Richard Whittington was Mayor of London, the City granted the Worshipful Company of Butchers a piece of land adjoining the Fleet River where they could clean 'the entrails of beasts'. In return they gave the Mayor a boar's head. This tradition, like polluting

rivers, continues to the present time. The Fleet became a sewer, though not due solely to the butchers, and runs below Farringdon Street into the Thames. Visitors may watch the procession as it leaves Butchers' Hall, 87 Bartholomew Close, EC1, down Little Britain, St Martin Le Grand and Cheapside.

CHRISTMAS

Christmas lights are switched on in Regent Street and Oxford Street in mid-November and in December the giant spruce, an annual present from Norway in gratitude for Britain's help in the war, is erected.

The new year is welcomed at Trafalgar Square in chaotic style by crowds of people with ambulances and police in attendance for the inevitable casualties. Parliament Square may be quieter where people gather to hear Big Ben ring in the new year.

'Andrew Lloyd Webber's best'

Daily Telegraph

Prince of Wales Theatre

Coventry Street, London W1

Box Office: 071- 839 5972

Credit Cards (24hrs/7 days + Bkg Fee): **FIRST CALL 071- 836 3464**

TICKETMASTER 071- 379 6131 KEITH PROWSE 071-793 1000

NOW BOOKING TO OCTOBER 1991
SOME TICKETS HELD FOR WEDNESDAY
MATINEE. APPLY TO BOX OFFICE

FOR THE BEST IN THE WEST END, FOLLOW THE SIGNS

ALBERY THEATRE
St Martin's Lane
London WC2N 4AH
Box Office: 071 837 1115
Leicester Square

PICCADILLY THEATRE
Denman Street
London W1V 8DY
Box Office: 071 867 1118
Piccadilly Circus

COMEDY THEATRE
Panton Street
London SW1Y 4DN
Box Office: 071 930 2578
Piccadilly Circus

WHITEHALL THEATRE
14 Whitehall
London SW1A 2DY
Box Office: 071 867 1119
Charing Cross

PHOENIX THEATRE
Charing Cross Road
London WC2H 0JP
Box Office: 071 240 9661
Tottenham Court Road

WYNDHAMS THEATRE
Charing Cross Road
London WC2H 0DA
Box Office: 071 867 1116
Leicester Square

MAYBOX GROUP PLC.
Albery Theatre
St Martin's Lane
London WC2N 4AH
Tel: 071 867 1122
Fax: 071 867 1131

PANORAMIC VIEWS

Opening times and admission charges were correct at the time of going to press but do check before you visit since they are subject to change at any time.

Alexandra Palace, Muswell Hill, N22
Stand on the terrace to get a view over four counties – Surrey, Kent, Essex and Hertfordshire.

Eltham Park, SE9
A wide panorama of central London can be seen from the top of the steps above the ornamental pond. Point Hill, Greenwich and Greenwich Park are nearby (see below).

Greenwich Park, SE10
Fine views from beside General Wolfe's statue and the Old Royal Observatory at the top of the hill over the Queen's House, Royal Hospital and the Thames to the Isle of Dogs and London. Afterwards you can straddle the Meridian Line, visit the museums and explore the *Cutty Sark* and 101 other things in Greenwich.

Hampstead Heath, NW3
Constable sat on Hampstead Heath to paint his famous view of the city. Find Jack Straw's Castle for a fabulous view of London from the north as far as the hills of Kent on a clear day. (You can get lunch and dinner in the restaurant, 12-2 and 6-12 Mon-Sat, 12-3 and 7-10 Sun. 071-435 8885.)

Heathrow Airport, Middlesex
From the roof of Queen's Building there are views of aircraft ceaselessly taking off and landing. Kids love it. At the time of going to press this facility was temporarily suspended so check opening times and charges (about 90p adults) with the airport. 081-759 4321.

Hungerford Foot Bridge, WC2
Dazzling views over the water at night – if you don't mind the sound of trains thundering over Hungerford Bridge – from Cleopatra's Needle to the Royal Festival Hall.

London Hilton, Park Lane, W1
Spectacular views from the roof bar across Mayfair, Hyde Park and Buckingham Palace. Lift. 5-12 pm daily. 071-493 8000.

Monument, Monument Street, EC3
If your legs can take it, climb the 311 stairs inside the pillar for a breathtaking view over central London. 31 Mar-30 Sept 7-6 Mon-Fri, 2-6 Sat & Sun; 1 Oct-30 Mar 7-4 Mon–Sat, closed Sun. Last admission 20 mins before closing time. £1 Adults, 25p Children. 071-626 2717.

Point Hill, Blackheath, SE10
A few minutes' drive from Greenwich Park (see above), this is another spot from which to enjoy a magnificent view over London, from Westminster (west) to Alexandra Palace (north) to the City (east).

Primrose Hill, NW3
The primroses are long gone, but on a clear day you will be able to see beyond Dulwich as far as Crystal Palace in the south-east. Druids perform pagan rites here at the autumn equinox (noon 23 Sept 1991).

St Paul's Cathedral, Ludgate Hill, EC4
A marathon climb up the 278 steps to the Golden Gallery is rewarded with panoramic views over the Wren churches, the Tower of London and the City. 7.30-6 Mon–Sat. Galleries closed Sun. Ring 071-248 2705 for admission charges.

Tower Bridge, SE1
High walkways provide unique views over London and the Thames. Apr-Oct 10-6.30, Nov-Mar 10-4.45 daily.

Last admission 45 mins before closing time. Closed 1 Jan, Good Friday, 24-26 Dec. £2.50 Adults, £1 Concessions, 5 and under free. 071-407 0922.

Waterloo Bridge, WC2

A river panorama that includes Westminster and the City, but you have to put up with the trains roaring in and out of Waterloo station.

Westminster Cathedral, Ashley Place, SW1

A lift takes you to the top for views over the Thames and Westminster. 7am-10pm daily.

RIVER ATTRACTIONS

Albert Bridge, SW11

This delicate Victorian cast iron bridge dates from the 1870s and is a beautiful sight when illuminated at night. It is a long-standing tradition that soldiers crossing the bridge must break step in case the structure is weakened by the rhythm of their marching.

HMS Belfast, Morgan's Lane, Tooley Street, SE1

There are seven decks to explore on this last surviving battle cruiser from World War II, including sick bay, gun deck and engine rooms. A novel way to get there is by Riverbus from Tower Pier. 20 Mar-31 Oct 10-6 daily, 1 Nov-19 Mar 10-4.30 daily. Last admission 30 mins before closing time. Closed 24-26 Dec, 1 Jan. £3.50 Adults, £1.75 Concessions. 071-407 6434.

Brunel Engine House Museum, SE16

The museum building was originally constructed to house the steam engines that pumped water from Isambard Kingdom Brunel's Rotherhithe Tunnel. You can see the tunnel, a remarkable engineering achievement of the 1880s, from Wapping Underground station, but for the museum take the East London line to Rotherhithe Underground station. 11-4 first Sunday in every month, £1.50 Adults, 50p Concessions, or by appointment on 081-318 2489.

Cutty Sark, SE10

In dry dock at Greenwich. Built in 1869, this is the only surviving tea clipper. On its runs to and from India it beat all contemporary speed records. Now lovingly restored as a museum, it contains the largest collection of painted figureheads in the world. Easter-30 Sept 10-6 Mon-Sat, 12-6 Sun, closed 1 hour earlier in winter. Allow at least an hour to get round. £2.50 Adults, £1.25 Concessions. 081-853 3589.

Docklands Light Railway

A part of the London Underground system. The trains run on a raised track through the heart of Docklands 5.30am-9.30pm Mon-Fri. A City extension to the Bank should be ready in 1992. Travel enquiries: 071-222 1234.

Gipsy Moth IV, SE10
In dry dock at Greenwich this tiny craft looks even smaller next to its awe-inspiring neighbour, the *Cutty Sark.* A tour of the boat is like a trip through a toothpaste tube – Francis Chichester deserved his knighthood just for putting up with the squeeze, apart from taking the craft on the first English solo trip round the world in 1966-67 at the age of 66. Easter-30 Sept. 10-6 Mon-Sat, 12-6 Sun. Closed in winter. 50p Adult, 25p Concessions. 081-853 3589.

Hammersmith Bridge, W6
Another decorative late-Victorian bridge, this one was built in 1887. It replaced the original 1820 Hammersmith Bridge, which was the first suspension bridge across the Thames.

South Bank Arts Centre, SE1
Spanning the ground between Waterloo and Hungerford Bridges, the 1960s concrete architecture is not to everyone's taste but inside is a whole new world. You can easily spend a day – or two – here. There are several bars, restaurants and bookshops, and in summer you can sit outside and watch the Thames on its journey to the sea.

The Royal Festival Hall was originally built for the 1951 Festival of Britain and is the venue for the world's top soloists and orchestras; more intimate pieces can be heard at the neighbouring Queen Elizabeth Hall and Purcell Room. Information on 071-928 3191.

The Hayward Gallery mounts spectacular large-scale exhibitions of contemporary and historical art. It closes between exhibitions but when open it can be combined with a visit to the nearby Museum of the Moving Image, National Film Theatre and National Theatre. 071-928 3144.

The National Film Theatre (three screens) is the place to go for classic films and there are seasons dedicated to individual countries or directors. 071-928 3232.

The National Theatre, designed by Denys Lasdun and built in 1976, is an interesting piece of modern architecture where you can sit in the early evening and listen to the free recitals by musicians in the foyer while you wait for the play to begin. The imaginative design allows the music to float upwards, permeating the whole building. Occasional narrow slit windows afford a fascinating glimpse of the Thames below. Home of the Royal National Theatre since 1976, the complex comprises three theatres: the Olivier, a large open-platform stage; the Lyttleton, a proscenium arch; and the smaller, more adaptable Cottisloe. Information on 071-928 2252.

Tattershall Castle
Floating bar moored near Charing Cross Pier. 11.30am-11pm daily. Disco in the Steamers Bar 11pm-2/3am Fri and Sat. In summer there's a bar on deck and a daily barbecue.

Thames Flood Barrier
The huge steel floodgates are supported by nine metal-capped concrete piers. Scale models can be seen at the Visitors Centre, Unity Way, Woolwich SE18. 10.30-5 Mon-Fri, 10.30-5.30 weekends. 081-854 1373. You can book a round-barrier cruise on 081-854 5555.

Tower Bridge, SE1
Built by Horace Jones and John Wolfe Barry in 1894. In summer the drawbridges, which weigh 1000 tons (1016 tonnes) each, are raised up to five times a day to allow large ships through. Precise times are available twenty-four hours in advance so ring 071-407 0922 for details or check the back page of *The Times*. The two towers house exhibitions showing the history, engineering and structure of the bridge. Apr-Oct 10-6.30 daily, Nov-Mar 10-4.45 daily. £2.50 Adults, £1 Concessions.

Westminster Bridge, SW1
Thomas Page and Charles Barry built this 80-foot-wide bridge in 1862. It is the best vantage point from which to see the Houses of Parliament and the Victoria and Albert Embankments.

MARKETS

There are street markets all over London; the following is
a selection of some of the better-known ones. For antiques
and bric-à-brac you'll get a better price if you offer cash for
two or three items at once; take a shopping bag (but keep
it out of sight – you don't want to look too enthusiastic!).
Wear flat shoes – the ground is often uneven and there
can be large puddles when it rains. Times given are
approximate as stallholders come and go as they please,
although generally within about an hour of each other.
Get there as early as possible.

Bermondsey Antique Market, SE1

Corner of Long Lane and Bermondsey Street. Reputedly
the largest antique centre in Europe, this is mainly a
dealers' market but visitors are welcome. It's besieged by
dealers at dawn so if you want to pick up a bargain, get
there at the same time – and haggle, as at all markets.
Silver, china, glass, objets d'art etc. 5-12 Fri only.

Berwick Street, W1

Just off Shaftesbury Avenue into the heart of Soho, this is
the place to go for fresh fruit and vegetables. You will also
find meat, fresh fish, cheeses and household goods. 9-5
Mon-Sat.

Brick Lane, E1

Part of Petticoat Lane market, this is the section for old
furniture and electrical goods. Officially 8-1 Sun but I've
been there none too soon at 7.30.

Brixton Market, SW9

Around Brixton Station Road. If you're into reggae you'll
love it. There's a strong Caribbean flavour to this lively
general market and the stalls are packed with exotic fruit
and vegetables, fish and meat. 9-5.30 Mon-Sat (Wed till
noon).

Camden Lock, NW1

By Regent's Canal off Chalk Farm Road. Tucked in
between the lock warehouses are scores of stalls selling

everything from bric-à-brac to designer clothes and pine furniture. Other stalls sell interesting food and cakes. The little craft shops along the edge are worth exploring too, but don't be surprised if you find a note on the door directing customers to the market pub, the Camden Head, where the shopkeepers have been known to conduct their business in a more relaxed atmosphere. Refreshments. 9.30-6 Sat & Sun.

Chelsea Antique Market, SW3
245-253 King's Road. Cheap, but scruffy, this friendly market is London's oldest indoor antique market. Men's clothes, watches, books and prints, theatre ephemera, scientific instruments etc. 10-6 Mon-Sat. 071-352 5689.

The Cut (or Lower Marsh), SE1
Off Waterloo Road (the Old Vic theatre is on the corner). A bustling general market that gets very busy when the local workers take their lunch break. 10-3 Mon-Fri.

Covent Garden Market,WC2
On the site of the famous wholesale fruit and vegetable market, which is now relocated at Nine Elms, SW8. Apple Market (antiques, bric-à-brac, open-air craft stalls) 7-7 Mon, 10-7 Tue-Sat, 9-6 Sun. Jubilee Market Hall covered market (antiques, bric-à-brac) 6-5 Mon; (general market, crafts, clothes, food) 9-5 Tue-Fri; (handmade crafts) 9-5 Sat & Sun. There's also a pedestrian shopping area where you'll find trendy clothes, restaurants and open-air entertainment.

London Bridge Collectors' Market, SE1
On London Bridge station. Coins, medals, militaria, postcards, stamps etc. 7.30-3.30 Sat.

East Street Market, SE17
Old-established general market with a wide variety of goods, and usually plants and fruit on Sundays. 7-5 Tue-Fri, 7-6.30 Sat, 8-2 Sun.

Greenwich Market, SE10
Burney Street. Antiques, jewellery, old records, clothes,

bric-à-brac and books. I rented a stall here myself one Sunday and the dealers crowded round to inspect my goods as I unpacked them at the crack of dawn. 8-4 Sat & Sun. Covered craft market, College Approach. Easter-Sept 9-5 Sat & Sun.

Leather Lane, EC1
Fruit and vegetables, groceries, clothes, crockery are on sale here but the main attraction is the noisy quick-witted banter of the stallholders. Some people go just for the entertainment – it's not unusual to see a whole dinner service tossed expertly into the air (and caught!). 10-2.30 Mon-Fri.

Petticoat Lane, E1
All around Middlesex Street, the stalls are packed with just about every kind of goods. There are specialist stalls in some of the side streets, eg bikes in Chilton Street (see also Brick Lane above). 9-2 Sun only.

Portobello Road, W11
General market 8-6 Mon-Fri (Thur 8-1), 7-6 Sat. The famous antique market is held 7-5 Sat, but it's not easy to make a 'find' these days.

PARKS AND GARDENS

Starting at the most northern open space in London, an invigorating walk over **Hampstead Heath** and **Highgate Ponds** could take in Kenwood (the Iveagh Bequest) and Keats' House, where he wrote 'Ode to a Nightingale'. The view over London from **Parliament Hill**, at the southern end of the heath, is spectacular. Here may also be kites weaving and bobbing against the clouds. Tea in Hampstead of course, leaving time to buy a 6-foot standard lamp with tasselled shade at a curio shop to take home on the bus in the rush hour.

REGENT'S PARK

Regent's Park, once a royal hunting ground, was planned by the Prince Regent (from 1820 George IV) to be part of his grand scheme for London, that included Pall Mall, the Theatre Royal, Haymarket and Regent Street – this last to link the royal park with Carlton House, the Regent's London home. The plan, designed by Beau Nash, was never completed though the crescents and stately terraces around the park show his hand.

The hub of Regent's Park is the intimate Inner Circle, reached by York Bridge with Regent's College to the left – the former Bedford College of the University of London. It

Regent's Park

is in this circle of Queen Mary's Rose Garden that the Open Air Theatre is held in the summer. There you can take a picnic and see 'The Tempest', or 'As You Like It' in a realistic 'Forest of Arden' setting.

The lake, with its bird sanctuary, is just west of the rose garden and was formed by damming the Tyburn River, one of the lost rivers of London, just as the Serpentine was formed in Hyde Park by damming the Westbourne River. A band plays here at the bandstand in the height of summer.

THE ARK IN THE PARK

Meandering pathways lead past the sports areas, refreshment pavilion and fountain to the south entrance of London Zoo, the home of the Zoological Society since it

was founded in the 1820s. The Royal Menagerie was moved here from the Tower of London in 1834 and now over 6000 separate species live here in pampered captivity, including the jet-setting giant panda whose services are required all over the world for propagating his endangered species. The polar bears have gone to a new home in Poland, but, to compensate, the zoo has the only koalas in Europe. Recent additions are a new aviary and invertebrate house. Animal feeding times and other events are staggered

London Zoo

throughout the day. There are limited facilities for wheel-chairs, which fortunately include disabled toilets.

Part of the zoo is reached by tunnel under the road and borders Regent's Canal. This waterway links the inland waterway system with the Thames and the sea via Regent's Dock in Docklands. There are canalside walks, not accessible from the zoo, and a canal bus from Little Venice, near Paddington, which includes zoo entrance in the price and stops right inside the zoo.

There is also a boarding place at the other end of the cut, at Camden Lock, where a thriving market is held on Saturdays and Sundays. It is possible to get the canal bus to the zoo from this end as well, and the prices are cheaper.

Kensington Palace

HYDE PARK

Hyde Park was also royal hunting territory. Now cars sweep through the middle where once the boundary wall stood between Hyde Park and Kensington Palace Gardens. At the Marble Arch end, near where Tyburn gallows used to stand, is Speaker's Corner, where anyone might have his, or her, say on Sundays. At the Hyde Park Corner end is Rotten Row, where horses still ride on the track made by William III in 1690 to link the palaces of Whitehall and

Kensington. It was in Kensington Palace that the young Victoria awoke to learn that she was queen. A formal sunken garden with a serene lily pond stands in front of the red-brick palace and the Orangery provides tea.

The statue of Peter Pan is by the Serpentine. North is the Italian Garden: south are restaurants and the Serpentine Art Gallery.

HOLLAND PARK

If you happen to visit Portobello Road for the market there, the trip could be combined with a visit to **Holland Park**, especially in the spring to see the Dutch and Iris Gardens or in June for the Rose Garden. The rest of the garden is 28 acres of woodland with birds from the country living in the heart of town. The house, a Jacobean mansion, was largely destroyed in the Second World War. Art exhibitions are held in the Orangery and the Ice House. This curious circular building was used before the days of the refrigerator to store winter snow, densely packed. The gardener would then barrow up chunks to the ice box in the kitchen when needed.

CHELSEA

The Royal Hospital, Chelsea, was founded in 1682 by Charles II for Civil War veterans, some say at the request of Nell Gwyn. It was designed by Wren with later additions by Robert Adam and Sir John Soane (architect of the Bank of England). The Chelsea Flower Show is held in May in its grounds. Both the Royal Hospital and its museum are open to the public and are free of charge. Wren designed the staircases with shallow tread for old legs, but wheelchairs hadn't been invented then and now residents themselves have some difficulty getting around.

STATELY PLEASURE DOME

Adjoining the grounds is **Ranelagh Gardens**, all that remains of the eighteenth-century pleasure park where there were gambling, dancing, music and masquerades. The young James Boswell came here with Lord Eglinton and a party: 'This is an entertainment quite peculiar to London. The noble Rotunda all surrounded with boxes to sit in and such a profusion of well-dressed people walking round is very fine.' The Rotunda was a vaulted room about 50 metres in diameter. Pictures show it looking rather like the Reading Room of the British Museum on the inside and the Royal Albert Hall on the outside. Other nightspots for eighteenth-century quality were at Kensington Gardens and at Vauxhall, across the river.

PHYSIC GARDEN

Further along Chelsea Embankment is **Chelsea Physic Garden**, begun in 1673 by the Society of Apothecaries for the study of medicinal plants and herbs. It is the second oldest physic garden in England. The first is at Oxford. Seeds from the cotton plants here were sent to Georgia to start the great cotton plantations. Primarily a place of horticultural research and study, the garden is open to the public on Sunday and Wednesday afternoons only, though subscribing Friends of the garden may visit during office hours throughout the year.

VILLAGE RETREAT

Chelsea has much to offer for a quiet browse. Many notable people have lived here since Henry VIII made it popular. The royal children played here in Henry's manor house, which was later bought by Sir Hans Sloane for his retirement. When he died he bequeathed his vast collection of curios from all over the world to the nation and they formed the basis of the British Museum, Natural History Museum and Museum of Mankind. The manor was demolished. George Eliot, who wrote *The Mill on the Floss*, lived at Cheyne Walk, the Rev. Charles Kingsley, author of *The Water Babies*, lived at the Rectory, and the Scottish historian and philosopher Thomas Carlyle lived in Cheyne Row, in a house now open to the public. He and his wife entertained Dickens and many other Victorian literary figures here. A statue to him stands in Cheyne Walk, not far from the statue to another of Chelsea's famous residents, Sir Thomas More (near the old church).

BATTERSEA

Across the river, **Battersea Park** was built in the 1850s on an area by the Thames once renowned for duels. The lake attracts waterbirds, and for keen gardeners there is a glasshouse, and small specialist displays include a garden for the disabled. An unusual feature of the park is the Buddhist Peace Pagoda. Set on the South Bank between Albert and Chelsea Bridges, the park also has sports facilities including an athletics track, boating on the lake, a small herd of deer and modern sculptures dotted about. There is a lakeside cafeteria and during the summer there are children's entertainments.

Imperial War Museum

DOING THE LAMBETH WALK

Near Lambeth Palace is the disused church of St Mary-at-Lambeth, the resting place of not just Captain Bligh of the *Bounty* but the Tradescants, father and son, royal gardeners in the seventeenth century. The **Museum of Garden History** is located here and part of the church-yard takes the form of a seventeenth-century garden with plants in period. The curator asks me to stress that the church no longer holds services, but exhibitions.

Other places to visit in this area are the Nightingale Museum at St Thomas' Hospital and the Imperial War Museum. I found St Thomas' so difficult to locate that I wrote and complained to the management. There are several large corporate-style buildings on the South Bank near Westminster Bridge. Any one of them could be the hospital. It's easier to find the Nightingale Museum than Casualty! Florence Nightingale started her nursing school at St Thomas' in the last century when the building was still in Southwark. See *Budget London* and *Family London* for details of the other St Thomas' museum —'the old operating theatre. The Imperial War Museum recreates life in the trenches, the Blitz and the Falklands and is set in a patch of peaceful greenery at odds with its aggressive image. The building was the old Bethlehem (Bedlam) Hospital.

GREENWICH

Moving eastwards, the view of the National Maritime Museum and the Queen's House at **Greenwich** from **Island Gardens** across the river at the Isle of Dogs is one

Queen's House

of the great sights of London. The 'Dogs' were not domestic quadrupeds but a corruption of 'dykes' – canals or ditches around which the docks were constructed. It isn't an island either, but a spur of land around which the Thames loops. At the southern end of the loop is the terminus of the computerised Docklands Light Railway, fully automated and wheelchair accessible (see Using London's public transport and Disabled in London sections for details).

From the gardens the foot tunnel (by steps or lift) goes leakily under the Thames to Greenwich, the site of the easternmost of the royal parks, all formerly hunting grounds. There is a wilderness here, children's playground and sports facilities. It was on the slope leading to the old Royal Observatory in 1894 that anarchist Martial Bourdin blew himself up with the bomb he was carrying in his pocket. His dastardly scheme was used by Conrad as the plot of *The Secret Agent*.

Royal Observatory

Gypsy Moth IV

Nearby Greenwich village has boutiques, antiques and nautical pubs and the nimble may scramble over the *Cutty Sark* and the tiny *Gypsy Moth IV*. A RiverBus from the pier is the best way to get back to central London.

EPPING FOREST

Further out of London to the north-east, **Epping Forest** has traditionally been the day in the country for London's East Enders. This is no tame park where tulips bloom as they are told. Yet to achieve a natural-looking habitat a great deal of subtle management is needed. The more wooded areas are to the north, with flats and ponds to the south. The whole is criss-crossed by roads and villages where some of the 'forest people' still exercise their ancient grazing rights, which permit them to graze their horses, cows, sheep or even pigs in the forest.

SYON PARK

Further out of London to the south-west is **Syon Park**, which can be combined with a day at Kew Gardens and

Richmond Park by those with stamina. Syon Park, across the Thames from Kew Gardens, was designed by Capability Brown, and here are the Great Conservatory (the first 'crystal palace' with its mature coconut palm), the 6-acre rose garden, and the London Butterfly House, with free-flying butterflies, giant spiders and smaller creatures. The Heritage Motor Museum is also on the site with the largest collection of British cars in the world. The house, the London home of the Duke of Northumberland, was converted into an imposing mansion by Robert Adam. There are different opening times and charges for the various features.

KEW

Kew is the jewel of the London gardens and a centre of botanical research, which the entry fee helps to fund. There are uncountable millions of plant specimens here and the largest seed bank in the world. If it's raining there is plenty to see indoors with glasshouses and exhibitions, the Orangery bookshop and a cafe.

Kew Gardens

RICHMOND PARK

Richmond Park, on the other side of Richmond from Kew, is approached by toiling up Richmond Hill. This is not where the 'Lass of Richmond Hill' lived as the song refers to Richmond in Yorkshire. The deer are seen best from horseback when rider and mount become part of the natural landscape. There is a formal garden at Pembroke

Lodge and the Isabella Plantation must be seen when the azaleas and rhododendrons are in bloom. The best view of the Thames from anywhere is seen from the vantage point on Richmond Hill.

Richmond Hill

Note that most places are closed around Christmas and may be shut on some Bank Holidays.

D Attractions with this logo make an effort to welcome the disabled. Other places are accessible with help. Usually the older buildings and museums are the most difficult. Phone for details. Popular attractions have a queueing system for telephone callers. You lose your place in the queue by re-dialling, so stay on the line.

Kenwood House (the Iveagh Bequest), Hampstead Lane, NW3
081-348 1286
Free. 1 April (or Easter) to September daily 10-6;
September to Easter 10-4
U Not very convenient for Golders Green, Hampstead or Highgate. Limited parking.
Bus 210 from Archway tube station on the Northern line
D Limited

Keats' House, Keats' Grove, NW3
071-435 2062
Free. April to October Mon-Fri 2-6, Sat & Bank Holidays

10-1, 2-5, Sun 2-5; November to March Mon-Fri 1-5, Sat
10-1, 2-5, Sun 2-5
U Hampstead and walk
Buses (to Hampstead) 24, 46, 168, 268

London Zoo, Regent's Park, NW1
071-722 3333
Adults £5.20, 4-15 £3.20, Concessions £4.30
Summer daily 9-6; winter daily 10-4
U Camden Town and walk, or Baker Street and 74 bus
D Limited, toilets

London Waterbus Company, Little Venice
071-482 2550
One-way ticket from Little Venice to London Zoo,
including admissions: Adults & Senior citizens £7.00, 3-15
£4.30
Summer services daily Easter to end September 10-5 on
the hour; winter services weekends and school holidays
10.30, 12 noon, 1 pm, 3 pm
Journey time 30 minutes to Zoo
U Warwick Avenue
Buses (to Royal Oak) 18, 36
D Phone, folding wheelchairs just possible, access by steep
steps

Kensington Palace, W8
071-937 9561
Adults £3.75, Children £2.50, Concessions £2.80
Mon-Sat 9-5, Sun 1-5 (last admissions 4.15)
U Queensway, High Street Kensington
Buses (to Palace Gate, Kensington Road) 9, 10, 33, 49,
52, 52A, C1
D Phone

Serpentine Gallery, Hyde Park, W2
071-402 6075/0343, Recorded information
071-706 0454
Free. Daily 10-5, Closes at 4 in darkest winter
U South Kensington, Lancaster Gate
Buses 9, 10, 33, 52, 52A, C1
D

Holland Park, W8
071-602 9483 for house and garden,

071-602 7344 for Ice House and Orangery
U Holland Park, High Street Kensington
Buses (to Commonwealth Institute) 9, 10, 27, 28, 31, 33,
49; (to Notting Hill Gate from Oxford Street) 12, 88
D Phone

Royal Hospital Chelsea and Museum, Royal Hospital Road, SW3

071-730 0161
Free. April to September Mon-Sat 10-12, 2-4; October to
March Sun 2-4 (museum closed in winter on Sunday
afternoons)
Guided tours for parties by arrangement with the hospital
adjutant
U Sloane Square
Buses 11, 19, 22, 39, 137

Royal Horticultural Society, Vincent Square, SW1

Recorded information 071-828 1744 for details of Chelsea
Flower Show, seasonal shows and competitions

Chelsea Physic Garden, 66 Royal Hospital Road, SW3

071-352 5646
Adults & Senior citizens £2.00, 5-16 & Concessions £1.00
End March to mid-October Sun & Wed 2-5
U Sloane Square
Buses as Royal Hospital
D Mostly, toilets

Carlyle's House, 24 Cheyne Row, SW3

071-352 7087
Adults £2.00, Children £1.00
April to October Wed-Sun and Bank Holiday Mondays 11-5
U South Kensington, Sloane Square; buses 11, 22, 19
down King's Road
Buses 39 along Cheyne Walk is best, or 11, 19, 22 down
King's Road

Museum of Garden History, St Mary-at-Lambeth, Lambeth Palace Road, SE1

071-261 1891
Free. Mon-Fri 11-3, Sun 10.30-5
U Lambeth North
Buses 3, 44, 76, 77, 159, 170, 507, 510
D

Florence Nightingale Museum, St Thomas' Hospital, SE1
071-620 0374
Adults £2.50, Children & Concessions £1.50, Families
(2+2) £5.00
Tue-Sun, Bank Holidays 10-4
U Westminster, Waterloo, Lambeth North
Buses as Museum of Garden History, or (to Westminster
Bridge) 12, 53, 76, 77, 109, 170, 171, 171A, 184, 196,
507, C1, D1, P11
D toilet

Imperial War Museum, Lambeth Road, SE1
071-416 5000, Recorded information 071-820 1283
Adults £3.00, 5-16 & Concessions £1.50, free on Fridays
Daily 10-6
U Lambeth North, Elephant and Castle (from Waterloo)
Buses (to Museum) 3, 44, 109, 159, 196, 510, or (to St
George's Circus) 1, 12, 45, 53, 59, 64, 68, 141, 171,
176, 184, 188
D Phone

Docklands Light Railway: 071-222 1234

RiverBus: 071-512 0555

National Maritime Museum, Romney Road, SE10
081-858 4422
Adults £3.20, Concessions £2.20
Greenwich 'passport' ticket to National Maritime
Museum, Queen's House, Old Observatory and *Cutty
Sark*: Adults £5.90, Concessions £3.90
April to September Mon-Sat 10-6, Sun 2-6
October to March Mon-Sat 10-5, Sun 2-5
BR Greenwich, Maze Hill (from London Bridge)
DLR Island Gardens, then foot tunnel
Buses 1, 177, 188
D Limited, phone

Cutty Sark, King William Walk, SE10
081-858 3445
Adults £2.50, Under 16 & Concessions £1.25
(children must be with an adult)
April to September Mon-Sat 10-6, Sun 12-6;
October to March Mon-Sat 10-5, Sun 12-5

BR Greenwich, Maze Hill (from London Bridge)
DLR to Island Gardens then foot tunnel
Buses 1, 177, 188

Gypsy Moth IV, King William Walk, SE10
081-858 3445
Adults 50p, Under 16 30p
Easter to October daily 10-5.30 (last admissions); closed
winter
BR Greenwich, Maze Hill (from London Bridge)
DLR to Island Gardens then foot tunnel
Buses 1, 177, 188

Syon House and Park, Brentford
081-560 0881
House: Adults £2.50 5-16 & Concessions £1.75
April to September, Sun-Thur 12-5; October Sun 12-5 (last
admissions 4.15)
Gardens: Adults £1.50 5-16 & Concessions £1.00
April to September daily 10-6; October to March daily 10-
dusk (rose garden admission by 10p turnstile)
Combined House and Garden: Adults £3.75, 5-16 &
Concessions £2.50
Motor Museum 081-560 1378: Adults £2.50, 5-15 &
Concessions £1.75
April to October daily 10-5.30; November to March daily
10-4
Butterfly House 081-560 0378, Recorded information,
081-560 7272: Adults £2.25, 5-14 £1.25, Senior citizens
£1.50
Daily 10-5, winter 10-3
BR Syon Lane (from Waterloo)
U Gunnersbury then buses 237, 267 to Brent Lea Gate
D Garden, not rose garden

Royal Botanical Gardens, Kew
081-940 1171
Adults £3.00, 5-15 £1.00 Concessions £1.50
Daily from 9.30, closing time varies with daylight
U Kew Gardens
BR Kew Bridge (from Waterloo)
Buses 7, 27
D

WEST END TICKETS

14 CHARING CROSS ROAD, LONDON WC2

071 240 2337 10 lines
FAX 071 836 5049

WE OBTAIN THE UNOBTAINABLE TICKETS

"MISS SAIGON"
"ASPECTS OF LOVE"
"LES MISERABLES"
"CATS"
"PHANTOM OF THE OPERA"

AND ALL WEST END SHOWS

ALSO ALL SPORTING EVENTS
WIMBLEDON   F.A.CUP   CRICKET
HENLEY REGATTA   ROYAL ASCOT

ALL CONCERTS
WEMBLEY   HAMMERSMITH,
LONDON ARENA   ALBERT HALL

FREE DELIVERY THROUGHOUT CENTRAL LONDON

SPORT

For spectator or participant sports and fitness activities London is second to none. Just a selection of facilities is listed here with the visitor in mind. For more details see *Time Out*, which has weekly information about what's on in London, or phone Sportsline, 071-222 8000, a free information service.

FIND THE BALL

Wembley provides much more than the venue for the Cup Final in May. The 100,000 capacity stadium – scene of the 1948 Olympic Games – holds international soccer and rugby league matches as well as the speedway championships and greyhound racing.

The indoor arena, seating 8000, hosts the Royal International Horse Show, ice shows, ice hockey, boxing, badminton, gymnastics, rock concerts and much besides. Normally on non-match days Wembley stadium gives guided tours round the stadium; these have been suspended because of redevelopment but should be offered again during 1991. Telephone the number at the end of this section for latest details.

The home of Rugby Football Union, which hosts international matches and the Oxford *v.* Cambridge match in December, is at Twickenham, reached by British Rail from Waterloo.

Thomas Lord was the groundkeeper when the Marylebone Cricket Club (MCC) played on what became Dorset Square, near Marylebone station. When the club moved he took the turf with him. **Lord's**, a mile further north in St John's Wood, is now the home of both the MCC and the Middlesex Cricket Club and test and county matches are played here in the summer as well as at the **Oval**, in Kennington, the home of Surrey County Cricket Club.

The **Museum of Cricket** is at Lord's with the original

'ashes' fought for in test matches between England and Australia since 1883 when two Melbourne ladies presented the England side with the ashes of a bail in a tiny urn. Guided tours include a visit to the Long Room in the Pavilion with its unparalleled view of the pitch. This is normally only open to club members.

A major venue in summer is **Wimbledon** with its thirty grass tennis courts, nine hard courts and two indoor courts. Here the All England Lawn Tennis and Croquet Club hosts the Lawn Tennis Championships Meeting, or simply 'Wimbledon', in the last week of June and first week in July. Finals are played on the Centre Court and tickets change hands many times before a final astronomical price is paid by a lucky purchaser. The club gains no benefit from this profiteering and plans are afoot to stamp it out. Be careful when buying tickets for a test match or tennis final that you have a genuine ticket sold by someone with the right to trade in them. The best view is obtained on television but you miss the strawberries and cream.

Adjacent to the Centre Court is the **Wimbledon Lawn Tennis Museum** which has nostalgic tableaux of tennis tea parties overdressed in period to illustrate the history of the game.

London parks provide the most convenient places to play many outdoor sports in London. The best plan is to enquire in person as they don't appear to have a central park office. There are some central indoor sports centres listed below. Golf can be played in Regent's Park and on public courses around London.

A LEG AT EACH CORNER

The **Derby** is the highlight of the flat racing season, on Epsom Downs in Surrey on the first Wednesday in June. There are too many people here for the day to be enjoyed to the full and pickpockets enjoy the day out too.

Royal Ascot, as its name suggests, is attended by members of the Royal Family in state coaches from Windsor Castle not far away. The meeting lasts almost a full week towards the end of June and is attended as a state occasion by anyone who is anyone, the women in outrageous hats and the latest fashions. The Queen and

Queen Mother own several horses and the Princess Royal occasionally competes in National Hunt races – over the sticks – in the winter.

Sandown Park and **Kempton Park** racecourses are closer to London and hold flat and National Hunt meetings all the year round. Kempton Park Boxing Day meeting is a good day out. There's no happy medium with catering facilities at race meetings. It's either champagne

and caviare in the striped tent, or burger and bun in the beer tent. The racecourse is the only place left in Britain where hats are commonly worn by both men and women. This is because of the British rain. Be careful if betting on the Tote. This mysterious system has rules of its own for paying out and the amount depends on the number of bets laid on the winner. For realistic odds go for the racecourse bookie in Tattersall's Ring, who is reliable but may have a minimum bet. There is no betting tax for bets on the course. Daily newspapers give details of the meetings.

There are riding stables near Hyde Park, Richmond Park, Ham Common and Wimbledon Common. Going east, a day in Docklands could take in a ride from the stables on the Isle of Dogs. See addresses below.

ON THE WATER

Fishing is free on the Thames as far upstream as Staines from boats and the towpath. All I ever caught in the Thames was roach, which even the cat wouldn't eat, but there have been reports of the occasional salmon and trout lately. Fishing in the parks, and the Pen Ponds in Richmond Parks, is allowed. Obtain a permit from the relevant park superintendent. Reservoir fishing is popular and day tickets and Thames Water Authority rod licences are available on site. The serious angler will already know of the London Anglers' Association, which can provide up-to-date information.

If I were a fish in the Thames I should burrow in the mud on boat race day. The race between Oxford and Cambridge Universities is usually held on a wintry Saturday before Easter from Putney to Mortlake. The scene is lively if you don't mind standing about until your toes freeze off but I prefer to watch it on television, even though my team keep losing.

There is tame boating in some of the London parks, and canoeing is offered by some sports centres, but the latest place for watersports is Docklands. The royal docks are very long and ideal for wetbiking and windsurfing.

Finally, don't forget Regent's Park Canal. Enquire at their information office for details of recreational activities.

The following list gives an indication of where various sports and leisure activities may be played. It is not exhaustive. Addresses and/or phone numbers are given at the end of the chapter.

Aerobics:
Chelsea Sports Centre, Dance Attic, Jubilee Hall, Kensington Sports Centre, Oasis, YMCA

Athletics:
Battersea Park, Crystal Palace, Kensington Sports Centre, Parliament Hill

Badminton:
Chelsea Sports Centre, Jubilee Hall, Kensington Sports Centre, Oasis, YMCA

Baseball:
Regent's Park (amateur)

Basketball:
Chelsea Sports Centre, Jubilee Hall, Kensington Sports Centre, YMCA

Bowls:
Chelsea Sports Centre, Hyde Park, Kensington Sports Centre, Parliament Hill

Canoeing:
Chelsea Sports Centre, YMCA
Cricket:
Kensington Sports Centre, Regent's Park,
Richmond Park, YMCA
Dance:
Chelsea Sports Centre, Dance Attic, Danceworks,
 Jubilee Hall, Pineapple, YMCA
Fencing:
YMCA
Fishing:
See addresses below.
Golf:
See addresses below.
Gym:
Dance Attic, Oasis
Gymnastics:
Dance Attic, Jubilee Hall, Kensington Sports Centre,
YMCA
Handball:
YMCA
Hockey:
Battersea Park, Jubilee Hall,
Kensington Sports Centre, Regent's Park
Ice skating:
Broadgate Ice Rink, Richmond Ice Rink, Queen's Ice
Skating Club
Jogging:
Hampstead Heath, Kensington Gardens, Regent's Canal
towpath
Judo:
Kensington Sports Centre
Karate:
Kensington Sports Centre
Kite flying:
Parliament Hill
Lacrosse:
Chelsea Sports Centre, Regent's Park
Martial arts:
Chelsea Sports Centre, Jubilee Hall
Netball:
Chelsea Sports Centre, Kensington Sports Centre, Regent's
Park
Riding:
Hyde Park: Richard Briggs, Ross Nye; Richmond Park &
Wimbledon Common: Wimbledon Village Stables;

Docklands: Mudchute Park
Roller skating:
Battersea Park, Chelsea Sports Centre, Kensington Sports
Centre
Rugby:
Battersea Park, Regent's Park
Sauna:
Chelsea Sports Centre, Dance Attic, Danceworks, Jubilee
Hall, Kensington Sports Centre, Oasis, Sanctuary
Skiing:
Beckton Alps
Soccer:
Battersea Park, Chelsea Sports Centre, Hyde Park,
Kensington Sports Centre, Regent's Park, Richmond Park
Softball:
Regent's Park (amateur)
Squash:
Chelsea Sports Centre, Jubilee Hall, Kensington Sports
Centre, Oasis, YMCA
Sub-aqua:
Chelsea Sports Centre, Kensington Sports Centre, YMCA
Swimming:
Open air ponds: Hampstead Heath (mixed and single
sex), Serpentine, Hyde Park; Indoor: Chelsea Sports
Centre, Crystal Palace, Kensington Sports Centre, Oasis,
Sanctuary, YMCA
Table tennis:
Kensington Sports Centre, YMCA
Tennis:
Battersea Park, Chelsea Sports Centre, Holland Park (no
advance booking), Hyde Park, Kensington Sports Centre,
Lincoln's Inn Fields, Regent's Park, Parliament Hill
Tobogganing:
Parliament Hill
Trampolining:
Jubilee Hall, Kensington Sports Centre, YMCA
Volleyball:
Chelsea Sports Centre, Jubilee Hall,
Kensington Sports Centre, YMCA
Watersports:
See addresses below.
Weight-lifting:
Jubilee Hall
Weight training:
Chelsea Sports Centre, Jubilee Hall,
Kensington Sports Centre, YMCA

Yoga:
Chelsea Sports Centre

Dance
Dance Attic, 212-214 Putney Bridge Road, SW15
081-785 2055
Danceworks, 16 Balderton Street, W1
071-629 6183
Pineapple Dance Centre, 7 Langley Street, Covent
Garden, WC2
071-836 4004

Fishing
Barn Elm Reservoirs, Merthyr Terrace, SW13
081-748 3423
Walthamstow Reservoirs, Ferry Lane, N17
 081-808 1527
London Anglers' Association, Forest Road Hall,
Hervey Park Road, E17 7LJ
Thames Water Authority, New River Head, Rosebery
Avenue, EC1R 4TP
071-837 3300

Golf courses (public)
18-hole
Brent Valley public course, Church Road, Hanwell, W7
081-567 1287
Trent Park, Bramley Road, Southgate, N14
081-366 7432
Richmond Park, Roehampton Gate, SW15
081-876 3205/1795
9-hole
Pickett's Lock, Edmonton, N9
081-803 3611

Ice skating
Richmond Ice Rink, Clevedon Road, Twickenham
(near Richmond Bridge)
081-892 3646
Queens Ice Skating Club, 17 Queensway, W2
071-229 0172
Broadgate Ice Rink, Eldon Street, EC2
071-588 6565 (tiny outdoor winter rink)

Riding
Richard Briggs Riding Stables, 63 Bathurst Mews, W2
071-723 2813, 071-706 3806

Mudchute Park and Farm Riding School, Pier Street,
Isle of Dogs, E14
071-515 5901/9271/4667
Ross Nye's Riding Establishment, 8 Bathurst Mews, W2
071-262 3791
Wimbledon Village Stables, 24a High Street, SW19
081-946 8579

Skiing
Mountain Top Ski Village, Beckton Alps, Alpine Way, E6
071-511 0351/2

Swimming
The Sanctuary, 11 Floral Street, Covent Garden, WC2
071-240 9635

Tennis
Lincoln's Inn Fields
071-405 5194

Watersports
East Docklands Watersports Club, King George V
Dock, E16
071-511 7000
Peter Chilvers Windsurfing Centre, Gate 6,
Tidal Basin, Royal Victoria Docks, E16
071-474 2500

Multi-sports and leisure centres
Chelsea Sports Centre, Chelsea Manor Street, SW3
071-352 6985/0366
Crystal Palace National Sports Centre, Anerley Road,
SW19
081-778 0131
Jubilee Hall Recreation Centre, Tavistock Street, WC2
071-836 4835/2799
Kensington Sports Centre, Walmer Road, W11
071-727 9747/9923
The Oasis, Endell Street, WC2
071-831 1804
Regent's Canal Information Office, 289 Camden High
Street, NW1, 071-482 0523
The Sanctuary, 11 Floral Street, Covent Garden, WC2
071-240 9635
YMCA, 112 Great Russell Street, WC1
071-637 8131

MAJOR SPORTING VENUES

Wembley Complex, Main Box Office, Wembley, HA9 0DW
Box office 081-900 1234, Wembley Update 0898 600500, Tours 081-903 4864
U Wembley Park
BR Wembley Complex (from Marylebone, not Sundays)
D Phone 081-902 8833 (main switchboard)
Lord's Cricket Ground, NW8
071-289 1611
Guided tours including Museum of Cricket, Lord's Ground, 071-266 3825
Adults £3.50 Concessions £2.00
Daily. Essential to book
U St John's Wood
D Toilets, limited access, phone
The Oval, SE11
071-582 6660
U Oval
BR Vauxhall
Twickenham Rugby Union Ground, Whitton Road, Twickenham, Middlesex
081-892 8161
BR (from Waterloo) Twickenham then 281 bus or walk
All England Lawn Tennis Club, Church Road, SW19
081-946 2244
U Southfields
BR Wimbledon (from Waterloo)
D Phone
Wimbledon Lawn Tennis Museum, All England Club, Church Road, SW19
081-946 6131
Adults £1.50, Children to 16 & Senior citizens 75p, Students £1.00
Tue-Sat 11-5, Sun 2-5, Bank Holidays vary
U Southfields
BR Wimbledon (from Waterloo)
D Access, toilets

London's FA clubs

Arsenal, Arsenal Stadium, Highbury, N5
U Arsenal, Highbury & Islington
Buses 4, 19, 236

Brentford, Griffin Park, Braemar Road, Brentford, Middlesex
BR (from Waterloo) Brentford
Buses 237, 267
Charlton Athletic, Selhurst Park, Whitehorse Lane SE25
BR (from London Bridge) Selhurst or Norwood Junction
Buses 75, 157, 197
Chelsea, Stamford Bridge, Fulham Road, SW6
U Fulham Broadway
Buses 14 down Fulham Road or 11,
22 down King's Road
Crystal Palace, Selhurst Park, Whitehorse Lane, SE25
BR (from London Bridge) Selhurst or Norwood Junction
Buses 75, 157, 197
Fulham, Craven Cottage, Stevenage Road, Fulham SW6
U Parson's Green
Buses 74, 220, C4
Millwall, The Den, Cold Blow Lane, New Cross, SE14
U New Cross or Surrey Docks then 225 bus down Trundleys Road
BR (Victoria to London Bridge line) South Bermondsey
Bus 225
Orient, Leyton Stadium, Brisbane Road, Leyton, E10
U Leyton
Buses 58, 58A, 69, 158
Queen's Park Rangers, South Africa Road, W12
U Shepherd's Bush
Buses 283, or (to Wood Lane) 72, 105, 220
Tottenham Hotspur, 748 High Road, Tottenham, N17
BR (from Liverpool Street) White Hart Lane
Buses 149, 279, 279A
West Ham United, Boleyn Ground, Green Street, Upton Park, E13
U Upton Park
Buses 58, 58A, 104, 147, 162, 238, 515
Wimbledon, Plough Lane Ground, 45 Durnsford Avenue, Wimbledon, SW19
BR (Holborn Viaduct) Haydon's Road
Buses 44, 77, 156, 220, 280

APPROVED

Eccleston Chambers
Hotel & Conference Centre

Eccleston Chambers, which has been in existence for over twenty-five years, is a private Hotel which overlooks a large stately square, located within a few minutes from Victoria Underground and mainline stations. The Hotel caters for the Tourist, Corporate and Family Weekend market.

All possible conference needs are provided to assist in the smooth running and organisation of your event. It is very important that seminars run perfectly.

Our professional team has all the expertise necessary to ensure that your functions and stay runs smoothly.

Spacious Single, Twin, Double and Family rooms are available, all of which have en-suite facilities.

All rooms have colour television sets, direct dial telephones, tea and coffee making facilities, hair dryers and trouser presses, and all

rooms are fully centrally heated.

English breakfast is served in the breakfast room and is included in the booking price, and for early departures the Hotel offers a self service continental breakfast.

TARIFF
Single room from £35.00 / Double room from £45.00
Twin room from £45.00 / Triple room from £50.00
Family room from £55.00
All prices are inclusive of VAT and English breakfast

Eccleston Chambers Hotel and Conference Centre
30 Eccleston Square SW1V 2NZ
Tel:071-828 7924/7925 Fax: 071-828 7924

ACCOMMODATION

The hotels below all charged £55 or under for a double room (with bath if available), bed and breakfast, on 26 October 1990. Phone for an update on prices. The majority of the hotels and guest houses listed here are in the Victoria area as this is the area most likely to be convenient for incoming travellers and for the tourist attractions mentioned in these books. The closer you get to the centre of town, the dearer the hotels become. An interesting exception is the Hotel Strand Continental, one of the cheapest of those below, which has rooms on the third to fifth floor in a very central location but no lift.

Each of the hotels has been visited by the London Tourist Board, who publish annually *Where to Stay in London* and *London Budget Hotels*, from which this list has been taken. For full information please obtain the latest booklet from LTB, 26 Grosvenor Gardens, SW1W 0DU, or telephone their information line on 071-730 3488. They will also make provisional bookings if you write well in advance, or you can telephone bookings with Access or Visa on 071-824 8844. Bookings can also be made through travel agents and airlines or in person at LTB Tourist Information Centres at Victoria station and Heathrow. If you are already in central London try the British Travel Centre at 12 Regent Street, SW1.

For hotels catering for the disabled, contact the Holiday Care Service, 2 Old Bank Chambers, Station Road, Horley, Surrey, RH6 9HW, 0293-774535, or the London Tourist Board Central Accommodation Unit, 071-730 3450.

Please note that accuracy cannot be guaranteed as unfortunately firms change hands, go bankrupt or close for a variety of reasons. No liability, therefore, can be accepted for loss, disappointment, negligence or other damage caused by reliance on the information below. So if you find on arrival that your performing sea lion is not permitted beyond the foyer, please don't blame me!

Cardiff Hotel, 5-9 Norfolk Square, W2 1RU
071-723 9068/3513/4500
U Paddington

Chester House, 134 Ebury Street, SW1W 9QQ
071-730 3632/7646 & 071-824 8444
U Victoria
Colliers Hotel, 97 Warwick Way, SW1V 1QL
071-834 6931/071-828 0210
U Victoria
Eaton House Hotel, 125 Ebury Street, SW1W 9QU
071-730 8781
U Victoria
Kerwin Hotel, 20 St George's Drive, SW1V 4BN
071-834 1595
U Victoria
Lewis House Hotel, 111 Ebury Street, SW11 9QU
071-730 2094
U Victoria
Luna House Hotel, 47 Belgrave Road, SW1V 2BB
071-834 5897
U Victoria
Magnolia Hotel, 104 -105 Oakley Street, Chelsea,
SW3 5NT
U Sloane Square
Margam House Hotel, 120 Sussex Gardens, W2 1UB
071-723 0528
U Paddington
Melbourne Guest House, 79 Belgrave Road, SW1V 2BJ
071-828 3516
U Victoria
Melita House Hotel, 35 Charlwood Street, SW1V 2DU
071-828 0471/071-834 1387
U Victoria
Muralyn Hotel, 143 Sussex Gardens, W2 2RY
071-723 7309
U Paddington
Olympic House Hotel, 115 Warwick Way, SW1V 4HT
071-828 0757
U Victoria
Hotel Strand Continental, 143 The Strand, WC2R 1JA
071-836 4880
U Aldwych/Covent Garden
Wigmore Court Hotel, 23 Gloucester Place, W1H 3PB
071-935 0928
U Marble Arch

LONDON TRIVIA QUIZ

1. Where did Churchill buy his cigars?
2. When and where does a lion eat cabbages and coins?
3. When is the Queen's official birthday?
4. Which park has an Iris Garden?
5. What is Rotten Row famous for?
6. In which coach does the Queen ride to open Parliament?
7. What do you do if you have toothache?
8. Who was the 'Duchess of Duke Street'?
9. Where did the nightingale sing?
10. Where can you watch the changing of the guard?
11. Who looks down on Trafalgar Square?
12. Where does the London to Brighton Veteran Car Run start?
13. The Oval is the home of which county cricket club?
14. Fortnum & Mason's is famous for what?
15. Where would you spend a rainy afternoon browsing through books?
16. What did Nell Gwyn call James I?
17. Frith Street is the home of which famous jazz club?
18. Tea at the Ritz, but how do you get there?
19. Where and when do you pay the most for strawberries and cream?
20. Which street is shady on both sides?
21. Which parade takes place in Battersea Park?
22. Where would you find a Beefeater?
23. If you are terrified by a pterodactyl, which boating lake are you on?
24. Where can you lose your shirt on a horse on Boxing Day?
25. Tropical butterflies flutter by – where?
26. The Museum of Cricket is at which cricket ground?
27. When and where can you stand waving a banner to classical music?
28. At what number in Doughty Street did Dickens live?
29. Where can you watch Shakespeare on the grass?
30. Which is London's largest theatre?
31. The Duke of Wellington belonged to which club?
32. Which London store was built from old ship timbers?
33. The Man in Grey is a ghost who walks in which theatre?
34. Where is Charlie Chaplin's statue?
35. Which church bells ring 'Oranges and Lemons'?
36. Where can you see hundreds of Punch and Judy shows at the same time?
37. You catch a water bus to the zoo from where?
38. What are Red Arrows?
39. Who rides in the gilded coach in the Lord Mayor's Show?
40. Where can you play with working models of all types of machines?

Answers on page 132.

NUMBER SIXTEEN

Four Victorian Town Houses form this exquisite hotel with the unique atmosphere of the home in the heart of South Kensington.

16 SUMNER PLACE, LONDON SW7 3EG
Tel: 071-589 5232   Telex: 266638
Fax: 071-584 8615

TRADITIONAL EVENTS

The London Tourist Board (LTB) publishes a list of traditional events each January to help plan your trip to the capital. Phone LTB on 071-730 3488 for exact dates. For events in the City call in or phone the information bureau in St Paul's Churchyard on 071-606 3030. Acknowledgements to LTB for supplying the information below (in October 1990). Note that all guidebooks are out of date in some respects by the time they appear, so do check with the relevant tourist body before setting out.

DAILY

Changing the guard: Horse guards leave their barracks in Hyde Park 10.28 am Mon-Sat, 9.28 Sun, for the ceremony at Horse Guards, Whitehall, at 11 am Mon-Sat, 10 am Sun. Changing the guard at Buckingham Palace is 11.30 daily April to end July and alternate days from August to approximately end March (not in wet weather).

NIGHTLY

Ceremony of the Keys: Tower. Write for tickets to the Governor, Tower of London, EC3N 4AB, with as many alternative dates as possible.

JANUARY

Royal Epiphany Gifts Service: 6 January at Chapel Royal, St James's Palace, SW1.
Charles I Commemoration: Last Sunday at Banqueting House and Trafalgar Square, midday.

FEBRUARY

Chinese New Year: Dates vary for celebrations in Soho.
Gun salute: 6 February. Commemorates Queen's accession to throne. Hyde Park at noon, Tower at 1 pm. (If 6 February is a Sunday, guns are fired on following Monday.)

MARCH

Oxford and Cambridge University Boat Race: On a Saturday on the Thames between Putney Bridge and Mortlake.
Bridewell Thanksgiving Service: Second Tuesday at St Bride's church, Fleet Street. Lord Mayor of London, in

robes, attends service at noon.

Oranges and Lemons Service: Third or fourth Thursday at church of St Clement Danes in the Strand, 3 pm.

Spring Equinox: Druids celebrate the equinox on Tower Hill at noon.

EASTER

Maundy Money: In 1991 this ceremony is at Westminster Abbey, but it moves to a different place each year.

Butterworth Charity: Morning service at St Bartholomew-the-Great, Smithfield, concludes with distribution of money and hot cross buns.

Easter Parade: Easter Sunday in Battersea Park.

Harness Horse Parade: Easter Monday in Regent's Park.

APRIL

Spital Sermon: First Thursday after Easter at St Lawrence Jewry-next-Guildhall. Lord Mayor, sheriffs, aldermen in procession from Guildhall, noon.

Stow Commemoration: St Andrew Undershaft, Leadenhall Street, EC3. Date varies.

Gun salute: 21 April, Queen's birthday (as February).

Tyburn Walk: Silent procession from Old Bailey to Marble Arch, last Sunday.

MAY

Historic Commercial Vehicle Run: First Sunday at Crystal Palace Park from 6.30 am.

Epsom Derby: First Wednesday on Epsom Downs, Surrey.

Dunkirk Veterans' Service: St Lawrence Jewry-next-Guildhall, EC2, 3pm. Date varies.

London Private Fire Brigades' target spraying competition: Guildhall Yard, noon on a May Saturday, also on a date in September.

Punch and Judy Festival: Covent Garden, followed by service at St Paul's, Covent Garden, second Sunday at 11 am.

Beating the Bounds: All Hallows-by-the-Tower, Ascension Day (sixth Thursday after Easter), 3 pm.

Every three years also at St Peter ad Vincula in the Tower, 6 pm.

Chelsea Flower Show: Late May at the Royal Hospital, Chelsea. Phone 071-828 1744 for recorded details.

JUNE

Trooping the Colour: Second Sunday in June to celebrate the Queen's official birthday. Horse Guards Parade, 11 am. Write for a maximum of two tickets before the end of February to the Brigade Major (Trooping the Colour), Headquarters, Household Division, Horse Guards, SW1A 2AX.

Beating Retreat and Sounding Retreat: In June on Horse Guards Parade. Tickets from the end of February from Premier Box Office, 1b Bridge Street, SW1A 2JR, 071-839 6815/071-836 4114.

Royal Ascot: Towards the end of June. Tickets from the Secretary, Grandstand, Ascot, Berks.

Gun salute: 10 June for birthday of Prince Philip. See February for details.

Pepys Commemoration Service: St Olave's church, Hart Street, EC3R 7NB. Write to the church for details of the service and the buffet lunch.

Election of sheriffs: Around midsummer at Guildhall. Write in advance for tickets to the Keeper, Guildhall, EC2P 2EJ.

JULY

Royal Tournament: Mid-July at Earl's Court. The Queen and other senior members of the Royal Family take the salute. Write from mid-March to Royal Tournament Box Office, Earl's Court Exhibition Centre, Warwick Road, SW5 9TA.

AUGUST

Gun salute: 4 August for the Queen Mother's birthday. See February for details.

Cart Marking Ceremony: Guildhall Yard at midday.

London Riding Horse Parade: First Sunday in August, Rotten Row. Phone LTB for the address of the current secretary of the parade to obtain entry form and details.

Notting Hill Carnival: August Bank Holiday and the Sunday before it.

SEPTEMBER

Autumn Equinox: Druids hold equinox celebrations at Primrose Hill.

Election of Lord Mayor: 29 September, or near, at Guildhall. Tickets from the Keeper, Guildhall, EC2P 2EJ. Punch and Judy Festival: Covent Garden.

OCTOBER

Judges' Service: First weekday in October, Westminster Abbey. Private function but procession to Parliament at about 11.45.

Pearly Harvest Festival: First Sunday at St Martin-in-the-Fields, Trafalgar Square, 3 pm.

Vintage Festival: St Olave's, Hart Street, EC3.

Harvest of the Sea: Second Sunday in October at either St Mary-at-Hill, EC3, or St Margaret Pattens, Rood Lane.

National Service for Seafarers: Nearest Wednesday to Trafalgar Day, 21 October, St Paul's Cathedral, 6 pm. Tickets from Hon. Sec., Annual National Service for Seafarers, St Michael Paternoster Royal, College Hill, EC4R 2RL.

NOVEMBER

Fireworks Night: Yeomen of the Guard still check the cellars of the Houses of Parliament prior to the State Opening of Parliament and all around the country bonfires and firework displays are held on or near 5 November.

Phone 071-730 3488 in October for London firework displays.

State Opening of Parliament: Early to mid-November. Not open to public but usually on television. Procession from Buckingham Palace at approximately 11 am.

London to Brighton Veteran Car Run: First Sunday in November. Starts Hyde Park Corner 8-9 am.

Lord Mayor's Show: Second Saturday of November. Procession in City from 11 am.

Remembrance Sunday Ceremony: Second Sunday in November, Cenotaph, Whitehall, 11 am.

DECEMBER

Boar's Head Presentation: Procession to Mansion House, in the City. Date varies.

CHRISTMAS

Christmas lights: Switched on in Regent Street and Oxford Street in mid-November.

New Year's Eve: Midnight in crowded Trafalgar Square, or Parliament Square to hear Big Ben ring in the new year.

Christmas lights

Bank Holidays	1991	1992
New Year's Day	1 January	1 January
Good Friday	29 March	17 April
Easter Monday	1 April	20 April
May Day Bank Holiday	6 May	4 May
Spring Bank Holiday	27 May	25 May
August Bank Holiday	26 August	31 August
Christmas Day	25 December	25 December
Boxing Day	26 December	28 December

USING LONDON'S PUBLIC TRANSPORT

When you visit London, the best way to get around is the Londoners' way – by public transport. Central London and the suburbs are well served by both bus and Underground networks, and the fully wheelchair accessible Docklands Light Railway has opened up the Thames-side areas east of the Tower.

The headquarters of London Transport (LT) is at 55 Broadway, SW1, above St James's Park tube station, which also houses the London Transport Travel Shop. This deals not only with tickets and London Transport enquiries but sells a wide range of LT merchandise, souvenirs and books. In addition, there are Travel Information Centres at the following Underground stations: St James's Park, King's Cross, Liverpool Street, Oxford Circus, Piccadilly Circus and Heathrow. There are other LT Travel Information Centres at Victoria station and Euston British Rail, at West Croydon bus station and at all Heathrow terminals. See the London Transport services section for further details. Phone 071-222 1234 for travel enquiries and Travelcheck on 071-222 1200 for regularly updated travel information.

UNDERGROUND

The **Underground**, or tube, is the most comprehensive subway network in the world. It's fast and convenient – unless you're in a wheelchair. If this is the case see Disabled in London section for advice on transport in London. There are eleven Underground lines including the Docklands Light Railway, each with its own colour code. See the journey planner on the back cover. Smoking is banned everywhere on the Underground system.

DOCKLANDS LIGHT RAILWAY

The **Docklands Light Railway** (DLR) was opened in 1987, and runs in a Y-shape from Tower Gateway and Stratford down to a terminus at Island Gardens on the Isle of Dogs, where there is a DLR visitor centre. Extensions are planned to Bank in the City and to Beckton, beyond the eastern Royal Docks.

The service is fully automated with trains running

every few minutes. The main station is at Tower Gateway where there is a small information office (open 10–4 Mon–Fri only). Ticket machines take coins rather than notes so be sure to have plenty of change. Travelcards are valid on the service (see opposite for details).

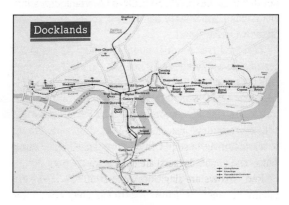

BUSES

Buses are no longer all red but those that aren't can be recognised as part of the London Transport system by the familiar roundel that they all carry. If you are sightseeing you may not want to go the fastest way, by tube, choosing instead to catch some sights on the way. Buses to the central attractions covered in this book are indicated in the individual chapters. If you take the number 11, for example, it  will take you from Liverpool Street station through the City, past St Paul's, Trafalgar Square, Westminster Abbey and down the King's Road to Chelsea. Or try the number 188 from Euston, which goes to Greenwich via the British Museum and the South Bank arts complex, and passes close to Tower Bridge. Free bus maps and guides are obtainable at LT's Travel Information Centres.

Buses have their own intriguing history. For instance, the bottom deck of a double-decker is still called 'inside', recalling the days when the top was open to the weather. See the London Transport Museum in Covent Garden for their fascinating collection of historic vehicles, posters and memorabilia.

Most **bus stops** in central London are named on the post or shelter and carry travel information. There are two kinds of stops: the compulsory stop, red on a white background, and the request stop, white on a red background. To hail the bus put out an arm. The driver will not stop if the bus is full. Sometimes it's wise to hail a bus at the compulsory stop, especially at night, in case the driver hasn't seen you.

Buses with a conductor are double-deckers (usually boarded at the back) and the conductor will tell you where to get off if you ask. Ring the bell in good time just once

to tell the driver to stop. Driver-only-operated buses (both single- and double-deckers) are boarded at the front.

Red Arrows are single-deck buses (501-513) running mainly between British Rail stations. They are driver-operated buses with a flat fare, currently 70p. Exact money is needed and the driver cannot give change.

Carelink and **Mobility** Buses are run by LT for the disabled, see Disabled in London section for details.

Night buses all pass through Trafalgar Square and serve main cinema, restaurant and theatre areas in central London until the day buses start. They have an N in front of the route number. For full details phone 071-222 1234.

BUYING YOUR TICKET

One-journey bus tickets are bought on the bus and one-journey single or return tickets on the tube are bought at the station of departure. Keep your ticket until the end of the journey in case an inspector is travelling on your route.

London is divided into six travel zones, from zone 1 in the central area to zone 6 in the suburbs. Bus passes are available in different combinations of zones for a week, a month or three months. They are valid at any time of day and are used by London's commuters. Buy them from certain bus garages, selected newsagents and Travel Information Centres. You will need to take a passport-type photograph along with you.

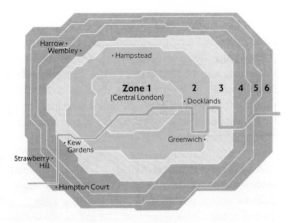

One-day, 7-day, monthly and 3-monthly Travelcards are valid for bus, Mobility Bus, tube and DLR, and for Network SouthEast (the British Rail suburban system). They are not valid on the Airbus or on guided coach tours. The 1-day Travelcards are valid after 9.30 am on Mondays to Fridays, and all day at weekends. They are not valid on the night buses. Travelcards are for sale at tube stations, Travel Information Centres and some newsagents. For all Travelcards except the 1-day you will need to present a passport-type photo when you buy.

AUTOMATIC MACHINES

There are self-service **ticket machines** in most tube stations to save a long wait. Follow the instructions on the machines. The larger style of machine displays the prices and zones. The smaller machine can be used if you know the fare. Both types accept coins from the 5p piece to the £1 and give change. The larger machine accepts the £5 note in good condition. Be sure to keep plenty of change to hand. **Ticket gates** are also automated. To enter the tube system slide the  ticket with the wording uppermost into the slot on the right-hand side of the gate. The gate opens when you remove your ticket. Leave the station in the same way – the ticket is returned to you if it is valid for another journey.

GETTING TO THE AIRPORT

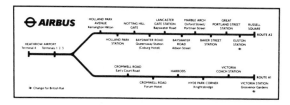

The wheelchair accessible **Airbus** links the major hotel areas with **Heathrow** every half-hour from approximately 6.30 am until 8 pm. The tube (Piccadilly Line) also links central London with Heathrow, and the journey takes about an hour. At night, bus N97 runs hourly between central London and Heathrow.

Gatwick is served by the Gatwick Express from Victoria British Rail station every 15 minutes from 5.30 am to 10 pm. The journey time is 30 minutes non-stop. Less frequent trains run overnight. You can check your luggage in at Victoria for some flights from Gatwick; ring first to find out (0293 31299).

DISABLED IN LONDON

It is possible to see many of the sights of London with careful advance planning. Most major museums and tourist attractions are improving their facilities for the disabled all the time and welcome wheelchairs, especially if you telephone first. Madame Tussaud's have to limit the number of wheelchairs they permit in case of fire, so do phone there before you set out. Phone numbers are given in the information sections for each itinerary.

Getting into London from Heathrow is not difficult by wheelchair as there are frequent wheelchair accessible **Airbuses** from Heathrow to Victoria and Euston stations that stop at several hotels on routes A1 and A2. Phone London Transport (LT) on 071-222 1234 for travel information. Leave out the 071 prefix if you are dialling from a number that has an 071 prefix.

The clockwise **Carelink** wheelchair bus run by LT runs hourly every day and connects up seven main railway termini: Euston, St Pancras, King's Cross, Liverpool Street, Waterloo, Victoria and Paddington. The driver may be able to make extra stops with advance notice as long as the timetable can be kept to. Phone LT's Unit for Disabled Passengers on 071-222 5600 for further information.

LT run **Mobility Buses** regularly to help the disabled in the suburbs do their shopping. Standard bus fares are charged as if the service were a regular bus. The most useful bus for visitors is Route 925 which runs on Wednesdays only from the East End. It arrives at Tower Gateway at 10.20 and stops at Liverpool Street, King's Cross, Euston, Oxford Circus, Marble Arch, Hyde Park Corner and Victoria station (at 11.40). The return trip leaves the Wilton Road coach station (Victoria) at 13.45 and arrives back at Liverpool Street at 15.00 before heading out to the East End. Phone 071-222 5600 for details.

The **Original London Transport Sightseeing Tour** has special wheelchair accessible tours from Wilton Road coach station (Victoria) on Saturdays, Mondays and Thursdays. Phone 071-828 7395 for information and booking.

The **Docklands Light Railway** (DLR) is completely automated with trains that are fully accessible for wheelchairs (two per train). An emergency button on the trains and platforms connects with the control room in case of difficulties. Automatic ticket machines take coins rather than notes, so be sure to have plenty of change on you. Travelcards are valid on the DLR as it is part of LT. Note that the 925 Mobility Bus stops at Tower Gateway DLR station on Wednesdays. Travel enquiries on the usual LT number 071-222 1234 (queuing system so hang on); leaflets from 071-222 5600.

The **Underground** is the least preferred option by wheelchair users and non-folding wheelchairs cannot be accommodated at all times on many sections. LT publish *Access to the Underground* to help, but steps are everywhere.

Disabled **car parking** is available in several places on the outer edges of inner London. Phone *Tripscope* on 081-994 9294 in office hours for free information on getting around anywhere in London. There are several useful phone numbers for the disabled in London (see below for a selection), but with the charity *Tripscope* you tap into the 'disability mafia' – the network of London disabled who know all the wheezes and short cuts because they live here.

Roving **taxis** are becoming more and more wheelchair accessible, especially from ranks where the adapted cabs are more easily spotted. If you are unlucky try the following numbers and ask for a taxi which can take a wheelchair, giving as much notice as possible:

Black Radio Taxis	081-209 0266
Data Cab	071-727 7200
Computer Cab	071-286 7009
Lords Radio Taxis	071-253 5000
Radio Taxis	071-272 0272

or phone *Tripscope* (who kindly provided these numbers) for an up-to-date list.

An independent guide to getting around London is *Access in London*, published by Nicholson in 1989, which has details of steps and toilets and much more.

For a RADAR key to disabled toilets and other information phone in office hours or write to the Royal Association for Disability and Rehabilitation (RADAR), 25 Mortimer Street, W1, 071-637 5400.

Other useful numbers are: Disabled Living Foundation, 071-289 6111; Greater London Association for the Disabled (GLAD), 071-274 0107; Disability Action Westminster, 071-630 5994; and Artsline (for arts and entertainment access), 071-388 2227.

LT's Unit for Disabled Passengers will send a comprehensive package of up-to-date London Transport information (in large print or on cassette if wished). Phone 071-222 5600 in office hours or write to them at 55 Broadway, SW1H 0BD. The London Transport Museum, in the corner of Covent Garden, is fully accessible for wheelchairs, with free admission for the disabled and their helpers.

LONDON TRAVEL SERVICES

The **Travel Information Service** is London Transport's shop window. It exists to provide passengers and potential passengers with helpful advice and guidance about every aspect of travelling around London – by bus, by tube, by the Docklands Light Railway and by British Rail. It can also give general information about the London tourist scene. Details of the location and opening times of Travel Information Centres are given below. Alternatively ring 071-222 1234.

TRAVEL INFORMATION CENTRES

These are open at Underground stations, Heathrow Airport and West Croydon bus station as follows:

	Mon-Fri	Saturday	Sunday
Euston (BR Concourse)	07.15-18.00 (to 19.30 Fri)	07.15-18.00	08.15-18.00
King's Cross	08.15-18.00 (to 19.30 Fri)	08.15-18.00	08.15-18.00
Liverpool Street	09.30-18.30	08.30-18.30	08.30-15.30
Oxford Circus	08.15-18.00	08.15-18.00	CLOSED
Piccadilly Circus	08.15-18.00	08.15-18.00	08.15-18.00
St James's Park	09.00-17.30	CLOSED	CLOSED
Victoria (BR Concourse – opposite Platform 8)	08.15-21.30	08.15-21.30	08.15-21.30
Heathrow 1,2,3 (station)	07.15-18.30	07.15-18.30	08.15-18.30
Heathrow Terminal 1	07.15-22.15	07.15-21.00	08.15-22.00
Heathrow Terminal 2	07.15-21.00	07.15-21.00	08.15-22.00
Heathrow Terminal 3	06.30-13.15	06.30-13.15	08.15-15.00
Heathrow Terminal 4	06.30-18.30	06.30-18.30	08.15-18.30

West Croydon bus station
Mon 07.00-19.00, Tue-Fri 07.30-18.30,
Sat 08.00-18.30, Sun closed

24-hour travel information: 071-222 1234

Travelcheck recorded information: 071-222 1200

For information by post, write to Travel Information Service, London Transport, 55 Broadway, London SW1H 0BD.

Free maps and leaflets Tourist information folders and Underground maps, along with a range of other free leaflets, are available at Travel Information Centres and most hotels.

Bargain Tickets and Tourist Services Ask at Underground stations and Travel Information Centres for prices and availability of Travelcards and bus passes.

The Original London Transport Sightseeing Tour and **Official guided coach tours** See pages 124 and 125 and ask for free leaflets at Travel Information Centres.

London Transport Museum, The Piazza, Covent Garden; open daily except 24, 25 and 26 December 10 am to 6 pm (last admission 5.15 pm). Come and see the many colourful and historic displays including horse buses, motor buses, trams, trolleybuses and railway vehicles. The museum shop (entrance free) stocks a wide range of books, posters, postcards and unusual souvenirs.

USING THE TELEPHONE

Central London numbers begin with the prefix 071- and outer London numbers begin with 081-. Central London is the area within four miles of Charing Cross. You do not need to dial the prefix if the number you are phoning from already has the same prefix. If you have any difficulty dial 100 and the operator will help you.

Phone boxes take 10p, 20p, 50p and £1 coins and the display tells you to 'insert coin' before you begin to dial. Unused coins are returned. Some phone boxes take phonecards only. These can be bought from post offices and newsagents' shops and cost £2, £4, £10 and £20. If you want directory enquiries dial 142 for London postal addresses and 192 for other British addresses. If you are phoning abroad dial 190 for general enquiries or 153 for directory enquiries. The direct dialling code out of Britain begins 010-.

Some telephone boxes now take credit cards. Instructions are displayed in the individual boxes.

HELP IN AN EMERGENCY

For emergencies dial 999 for police, fire brigade or ambulance. The call is free from any telephone.

Bliss chemists at Marble Arch are open till midnight every day of the week. Their telephone number is 071-723 6116.

British Transport Police, for reporting crimes on London Transport, are on 071-222 5600.

If you need hospital treatment in central London try University College Hospital, Gower Street, WC1; Middlesex Hospital, Mortimer Street, W1; St Mary's Hospital, Praed Street, W2; St Thomas' Hospital, Lambeth Palace Road, SE1, or Westminster Hospital, Horseferry Road, SW1.

Emergency dental treatment can be obtained at a charge from the Emergency Dental Service, 081-677 6363.

Property lost on buses or tubes may find its way to the Lost Property Office at 200 Baker Street, NW1 5RZ, near Baker Street tube station. The office is open on Mondays to Fridays 9.30 to 2 pm. For lost property recorded information ring 071-486 2496. For other lost property apply to the nearest police station.

TOURIST INFORMATION

London Tourist Board and Convention Bureau
26 Grosvenor Gardens, SW1W 0DU, 071-730 3450

Information centres at:
Victoria station Forecourt
SW1: open Easter to October daily 9-8.30 pm; November to Easter Mon-Sat 9-7 pm, Sun 9-5 pm

Harrods
Knightsbridge, SW1 (fourth floor): open during store hours

Heathrow Airport
Terminals 1, 2, 3, Underground station Concourse: open daily 9-6 pm; Terminal 2 Arrivals Concourse, open daily 9-7 pm

Selfridges
Oxford Street, W1 (Basement Services Arcade); open during store hours

Tower of London
West Gate, EC3; open Easter to October daily 10-6 pm

Telephone information service
071-730 3488 Mon-Fri 9-6 pm (automatic queuing system)

British Travel Centre
12 Regent Street, Piccadilly Circus, SW1Y 4PQ, 071-730 3400: open Mon-Fri 9-6.30 pm, Sat & Sun 10-4 pm (extended in summer)

City of London Information Centre
St Paul's Churchyard, EC4, 071-606 3030, for information relating to the square mile of the City of London: open May to September daily 9.30-5 pm; October to April Mon-Fri 9.30-5 pm, Sat 9.30-12 noon.

Bureaux de Change
Banks are normally open Mon-Fri 9.30-3.30 pm. Other exchange facilities can be found at mainline railway stations, central Underground stations and in some larger department stores. They may have longer opening hours than banks.

THE ORIGINAL LONDON TRANSPORT
SIGHTSEEING TOUR

Take an introductory look at London with the Original
London Transport Sightseeing Tour – open top in good
weather. You pass all the major central London attractions:
Tower Bridge, Tower, St Paul's Cathedral, Piccadilly Circus, Trafalgar Square, Houses of Parliament and Big Ben,
travelling along some of London's famous streets: Fleet
Street, Strand, Park Lane and around Hyde Park Corner.

Guided tours in English go from Piccadilly Circus
(Haymarket, Stop L), Victoria station (Victoria Street, Stop
T) and Marble Arch (Park Lane, Stop Z) every 30 minutes
daily from 10 am until 4 pm (except at 1.30 pm).

A tour with taped commentary in English, Dutch,
French, German, Italian, Japanese, Spanish and Swedish
leaves the forecourt of Baker Street Underground station
at the same times. Note that the times shown are only a
guide and are subject to alteration to meet demand. Where
possible, the departures on the hour are maintained.

Combined tickets to save queuing at Madame Tussaud's,
London Zoo and Rock Circus are available from sales
agents listed below and from departure points, except that
the Madame Tussaud's ticket is not sold at Baker Street:

- Porters' desks at many hotels
- London Coaches Wilton Road coach station, Victoria
- London Transport Travel Information Centres
- London Tourist Board Information Centres
- American Express Desk at the British Travel Centre,
  12 Regent Street W1.

Tours information
071-227 3456.
For wheelchair accessible tours see the Disabled in
London section or phone 071-828 7395.

OFFICIAL GUIDED COACH TOURS

Because London Transport knows the best way to see the
sights, they have assembled an exciting programme of
guided tours, carefully selected to show you places that
have played an important part in England's history.

On each tour you travel in a modern luxury coach and

are escorted by a friendly and experienced guide who has an expert knowledge of the places you will visit, and is approved to the high standard of the London Tourist Board.

A London Transport guided tour is a wonderful day out. On each day tour you can enjoy a relaxing lunch, and the price of all tours includes admissions charges.

SUMMER PROGRAMME
London Tours

Day tours
Westminster and City including changing of the guard and the Tower; river tour to Hampton Court Palace.

Morning tours
Westminster and changing of the guard.

Sunday luncheon cruise
Sights of London/changing of the guard/lunch cruising to Greenwich.

Afternoon tours
City of London; river cruise to Hampton Court Palace or Windsor.

Evening tours
Romance of London including dinner cruise; escorted theme evenings.

Country Tours

Day tours
Leeds Castle; Stonehenge, Longleat and Bath; Stratford, Oxford, Bladon and the Cotswolds; Stratford and Warwick Castle; Boulogne.

Extended tours
Visit England's lovely cathedral cities and towns, Lake District, Stonehenge, Bath, Shakespeare country, Devon and Cornwall, Scotland, Wales and Ireland.

Tours pick up from most major hotels. For full details ask for a free leaflet at Travel Information Centres or phone 071-222 1234.

BEWARE OF PICKPOCKETS

Keep an eye on your money and credit cards in crowded areas. Men should know how foolish it is to put wallets in their back trouser pockets. Beware of being jostled in a queue as some pickpockets work in groups. Women should beware of bag snatchers. Thieves watch you withdraw cash then follow you discreetly. Sooner or later your attention slips and the bag disappears. Hook your bag handle round your ankle in restaurants and hang it on a hook in the Ladies if there is a gap under the door. Another villainous trick is to slice through shoulder bag straps with a razor-blade.

Always lock your car and hide valuables under the seat or in the boot (trunk). Don't drive with a handbag or camera on the passenger seat if the window is open. Enterprising thieves on bikes can hook them away and leave you fuming in the traffic.

ASTON'S ™

Aston's offer the most complete selection of accommodation, each range uniquely tailored to fit your budget and needs. Aston's is centrally located just minutes from Harrods, Hyde Park, Buckingham Palace, Theatres and Museums. For reservations or more information please contact us. We'll look forward to your stay.

ASTON'S
BUDGET STUDIOS ™

From just
£25
a day

By combining self-catering convenience with elegant Victorian surroundings, our Aston's Budget Studios are quite simply the best of budget.

ASTON'S
DESIGNER STUDIOS™

From just
£55
a day

We offer glorious designer decor, the finest amenities and service. Marble showers, Gold Fittings, Robes, Opulent Mirrors, Air Conditioning, Private Fax & Phone. Truly a luxury you can afford.

ASTON'S
LUXURY APARTMENTS ™

From just
£95
a day

Tired of hotels? Our luxury apartments are a charming combination of old world elegance and modern sophistication. Really a home away from home.

39 ROSARY GARDENS, LONDON SW7 4NQ.
TEL: 071-370 0737 & 071-730 1100   FAX: 071-730 2382 & 071-835 1419

TOLL FREE (USA ONLY) 1 800 525 2810

PRACTICAL INFORMATION

Emergencies

You don't need any money – emergency calls are free. Dial 999 and ask for Fire, Police or Ambulance. State clearly the phone number given on the phone, the address where help is needed, what has happened and, if you know, how many people are injured.

SAFE AND SECURE

London is a comparatively safe city. Nevertheless, it is sensible to take precautions, especially in crowded places popular with tourists, and to keep a particularly careful eye on money, credit cards and personal possessions.

If travelling late at night, try to do so in a group of three or more and keep to well-lit main streets where possible.

Exchange

Chequepoint Bureau de Change
37 Coventry Street, W1. 071-839 3722.
13 Davies Street, W1. 071-409 1122.
220 Earl's Court Road, SW5. 071-373 9515.
Marble Arch, 548 Oxford Street, W1. 071-723 2646.

Eurochange Bureaux Ltd
95 Buckingham Palace Road, SW1. 071-834 3330.

In underground stations at:
Leicester Square, 45 Charing Cross Road, WC2.
071-439 2827.
Paddington, 179 Praed Street, W2. 071-258 0442.
Tottenham Court Road, W1. 071-734 0279.

Thomas Cook Ltd
123 High Holborn, WC1. 071-831 4408
104 Kensington High Street, W8. 071-376 2588.

Midland Bank
39 Tottenham Court Road, W1. 071-323 5445.
100 Victoria Street, SW1. 071-828 8985.
Selfridges, 400 Oxford Street, W1. 071-629 9188.

Taxis

You can hail one of London's famous black taxis in the street when the yellow light over the windscreen is lit up. The meter will show a minimum charge when you get in. There is an extra charge after midnight, at weekends, on public holidays, and for large luggage. If you can't find one in the street, ring:

Computer-cab 071-286 0286.
Owner Drivers Radio Taxi Service 071-253 5000
Radio Taxicabs 071-272 0272 (24 hrs).

Minicabs

Minicabs operate twenty-four hours a day and there are hundreds of companies (look in Yellow Pages).

Lady Cabs
60A Albion Road, N16. 071-254 3501. Cabs for women, driven by women. 7.45-12 midnight Mon-Fri; 7.45am-2pm Sat; 10-12 midnight Sun.

Self-drive car hire

Avis Rent-a-Car
68 North Row, Marble Arch, W1. 071-629 7811; 24-hour service from Heathrow and Gatwick airports.

Godfrey Davis Europe Car
Heathrow Airport. 081-897 0811. Desk in each terminal; 24-hour service.

Late-night chemists

Bliss Chemists
5 Marble Arch, W1. 071-723 6116. 9-12 midnight every day of the year.
50-56 Willesden Lane, NW6. 071-624 8000. 9-12 midnight every day of the year.

Boots
Piccadilly Circus, W1. 071-734 6126. 8.30-8 Mon-Fri; 9-8 Sat.
114 Queensway, W2. 071-229 8387. 9.15-10 daily.

Warman-Freed
45 Golders Green Road, NW11. 081-455 4351. 8.30-12 midnight every day of the year.

When the police can help

Dial 142, Directory Enquiries, for the number of your
nearest police station. In an emergency dial 999 (see
Emergencies, above).

Each police station keeps a list of:
local emergency doctors
local late-night chemists
local garages, with opening times
local hotels, with prices
lost property offices
The police can help if:
your car is stolen
your dog is lost
you need money to get home. If you're visiting London
from the provinces and you have spent all your money,
you can give the police the name of someone back home
who will deposit your fare at the local police station. The
London police will then give you a travel warrant to get
you home. (British residents only. Other nationalities
should apply to their own embassy.)

Help and advice

Citizens Advice Bureaux

33 Charing Cross Road, WC2. 071-839 2825.
There are Citizens Advice Bureaux all over the UK. Look
in the telephone directory under C for the one nearest to
you. Free, impartial, confidential advice to anyone on any
subject.

Capital Helpline

071-388 7575. Telephone helpline for all types of
problem. Leave your name and number on the
answerphone after office hours and they'll ring you back.
Very busy – keep trying.

International Traveller's Aid

Portacabin, Platform 15, Victoria station, SW1. 071-834
3901. A voluntary organisation connected with YWCA.
Gives advice to foreign nationals on many subjects,
including accommodation.

Office of Fair Trading, 15-25 Bream's Buildings, EC4.
071-242 2858.
Leaflets covering all aspects of consumer purchase, both
goods and services. These can also be obtained from
Citizens Advice Bureaux (see above).

Public toilets

Public toilets are signposted near all major tourist spots,
parks, pubs, museums, libraries and art galleries, at all
railway and coach termini, many Underground stations,
and all department stores. Few are open twenty-four
hours a day except the new unisex automatic 'cabinets'
that are appearing on the streets.

Automatic unisex toilets (entrance 10p, open 24 hours a
day):
Adelaide Street, WC2, off The Strand
Balderton Street, W1, opposite Selfridges, off Oxford
   Street (wheelchair access)
Bressenden Place, SW1, at junction with Victoria Street
Cambridge Circus, WC2, junction of Charing Cross Road
   and Moor Street
Hyde Park Corner, SW3, west side
Leicester Square, WC2, in the south-east corner
London Street, W2, off Praed Street
Lumley Street, W1, opposite Selfridges, off Oxford Street
Lupus Street, SW1, outside Littleton House
Marylebone Road, NW1, opposite Madame Tussaud's near
Baker Street Underground
Old Marylebone Road, NW1, near junction with Edgware
   Road
Paddington Street, W1, in the gardens
Pimlico Road, SW1, on Orange Square centre island
Soho Square, W1, north side
Tavistock Place, WC2, by Jubilee Hall and London
Transport Museum
Victoria Embankment, WC2, in the gardens by
   Hungerford Bridge
Walterton Road, W9, junction with Harrow Road
Wellington Place, NW8, in gardens near Lord's Cricket
   Ground

Public toilets with wheelchair access:

Balderton Street, W1, opposite Selfridges, off Oxford Street (automatic unisex, open 24 hours a day)

Embankment, WC2, by Embankment Underground (old-fashioned type), free, 7.30am-11pm daily

Greenwich Park. In the Avenue and the Rockery. Summer 7am-9.30pm daily; winter 7-6 daily

Holland Park. Near the Orangery. Summer 8-8 daily, winter 8-5 daily

Hyde Park. Two in the south-east corner (one near Hyde Park Underground), one opposite the bandstand); another in the centre near the Serpentine. Summer 7.30-8 daily, winter 7.30-6 daily

Kensington Gardens. One opposite Lancaster Gate Underground; one by the Serpentine Gallery near the Royal Albert Hall; one in the south-west corner near the Kensington High Street entrance; one in the north-west corner by the children's playground 5 till dusk, daily all year round

Marble Arch, W1, in the subway by the fountains (old-fashioned type), free, 7.30am-11pm daily

Regent's Park. On the south side by York Gate near Madame Tussaud's. Summer 7-7.30 daily, winter 7-4 daily

Westminster Bridge, SW1. By Westminster Pier (old-fashioned type), free, 7.30am-11pm daily

'Old-fashioned toilets'

Barrett Street, W1. On island 7.30am-11pm daily

Bayswater Road opposite Queensway, W2. 10-6 daily

Broad Sanctuary, SW1, by Westminster Abbey. 7.30am-11pm daily

Broadwick Street, W1 opposite Ingestre Place. 10-6 daily

Covent Garden, WC2, by the Piazza.7.30am-11pm daily

Edgware Road, W1, subway at Baker Street. 7am-11pm daily

Edgeware Road, W2, beneath underpass. 7.30am-11pm daily

Embankment, WC2, by Embankment Underground. 7.30am-11pm daily

Great Marlborough Street, W1, near Carnaby Street. 7.30am-11pm daily

Great Portland Street, W1, by Great Portland Street Underground station. 10-6 daily

Harrow Road, W9, on island junction with Walterton Road. 10-6 daily

Marble Arch, W2, in the subway by the fountains. Wheelchair access. 7.30am-11pm daily

Marylebone Road, W1, subway at Baker Street. 7am-11pm daily

Oxford Circus, W1, on the north side. 7.30am-11pm daily Paddington Street, W1, in gardens opposite Luxborough Street. 10-6 daily

Parliament Street, SW1, by Parliament Square in the subway. 7.30am-11pm daily

Piccadilly Circus W1 in the subway. Admission 10p. 7.30am-11pm daily

Pimlico Market, SW1, opposite Church Street. 10-6 daily

Queensway, W2, junction on island at with Bishopsbridge Road. 7.30am-11pm daily

Salisbury Street, NW8, on island in Church Street. 10-6 daily

The Strand, WC2, Wellington Street. 10-6 daily

The Strand, WC2, opposite the Law Courts, at the top of Fleet Street. 10-6 daily

Trafalgar Square, SW1, on the south side in Cockspur Street subway. Admission 10p. 7.30am-11pm daily

Victoria Street, SW1, Bressendon Place. 10-6 daily

Wellington Place, NW8, in gardens. 10-6 daily

Westminster Bridge, SW1, by Westminster Pier. Wheelchair access. 7.30am-11pm daily

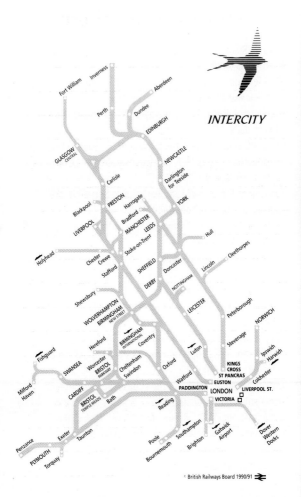

INTERCITY

< British Railways Board 1990/91 ≥

FOR YOUR PERSONAL USE

LONDON TRIVIA ANSWERS

1. Robert Lewis, St James's Street
2. During the Chinese New Year celebrations (February) in Gerrard Street
3. Second Sunday in June
4. Holland Park
5. Horse-riding
6. Irish State Coach
7. Ring the Emergency Dental Service (081-677 6363)
8. Rosa Lewis
9. Berkeley Square
10. Buckingham Palace, Horse Guards in Whitehall, and the Tower of London (also Windsor Castle)
11. Nelson
12. Hyde Park Corner
13. Surrey
14. Hampers and groceries
15. Charing Cross Road
16. Dismal Jimmie
17. Ronnie Scott's
18. Your chauffeur drives you in the Rolls – or you take the tube to Green Park station
19. Wimbledon during the Lawn Tennis Championships
20. Wardour Street
21. The Easter Parade
22. Tower of London
23. Crystal Palace
24. Kempton Park
25. London Butterfly House, Syon Park
26. Lord's
27. Last night of the Proms, Royal Albert Hall
28. No. 48
29. Regent's Park Open Air Theatre
30. Coliseum (seats 2400)
31. Athenaeum
32. Liberty
33. Theatre Royal, Drury Lane
34. Leicester Square
35. St Clement Danes in the Strand
36. The Punch and Judy Fellowship festival, Covent Garden (last Sunday in September or first in October)
37. Little Venice or Camden Lock
38. Single-deck buses that run mainly between railway stations
39. The Lord Mayor
40. Science Museum, Exhibition Road